The 20 British Prime Ministers
of the 20th century

First published in Great Britain in 2006 by
Haus Publishing Limited
26 Cadogan Court
Draycott Avenue
London SW3 3BX

www.hauspublishing.co.uk

A CIP catalogue record for this book is available from the British Library

ISBN 1-904950-58-2

Designed by BrillDesign
Typeset in Garamond 3 by MacGuru Ltd
info@macguru.org.uk

Printed and bound by Graphicom, Vicenza

Front cover: John Holder

Lloyd George

HUGH PURCELL

HAUS PUBLISHING · LONDON

Contents

Introduction

The young Welsh solicitor David Lloyd George was elected Liberal MP for Caernarvon Boroughs in April 1890. He retained the seat in 13 subsequent elections and held it for 55 years until his death in 1945. Considering the longevity of his parliamentary career and his unrivalled political supremacy for much of it, it is remarkable that he was only Prime Minister for one period of office. He was in the Cabinet continuously for 17 years between 1905 and 1922; first as President of the Board of Trade, second as a radically reforming Chancellor of the Exchequer and then as Prime Minister for six tumultuous years, 1916–22. No other prime minister of the 20th century except Winston Churchill had greater power, first as Britain's wartime leader and then as international architect of the peace treaties. After this supreme authority he never held a government post again. Yet, just as before his protracted period of public office he was a significant backbencher, so afterwards, for two decades in fact, he was a dominant figure in British political life.

What made Lloyd George unique was his remarkable political independence. Although he was a Liberal Prime Minister he depended on a largely Conservative coalition Cabinet and after he lost office he continued as an outsider, semi-detached from party politics. In the 1920s he might well have 'fused' a party of the centre, between the *reaction* of the die-hard Conservatives and the *revolution* of Labour (his words); at first, possibly, a new party and then under the Liberal banner. In 1929 he was poised to take power again at the head of a reunited Liberal Party with a raft of radical and novel economic policies. Had the electorate returned him to 10 Downing Street there might have been no financial crisis in 1931 and the dreary history of the 1930s with its mass unemployment and hunger marches might have been averted. Instead the Liberal Party splintered and he now became the elder statesman courted by the leaders of the other two. The Labour Prime Minister Ramsay MacDonald wanted a Lab–Lib alliance in 1931 and, it was supposed, offered Lloyd George the Treasury or Foreign Office. The Conservative Prime Minister Stanley Baldwin wanted him in the Cabinet of his National Government in 1935 and Winston Churchill invited him to join his War Cabinet in 1940.

For four decades David Lloyd George was the major catalyst for change in British politics, in peace and war. When he died in March 1945 Churchill said in the House of Commons: 'When the British history of the first quarter of the twentieth century is written, it will be seen how great a part of our fortunes in peace or in war were shaped by this one man.'

He was a hugely important figure and hugely controversial. In his lifetime his reputation changed from one extreme to the other, from hero to scapegoat. Until 1920 he was the 'People's David', a British Abraham Lincoln who championed the poor against the rich and became 'the man who won the war'. Then he was knocked off his pedestal. In the 1920s he was hated as an unprincipled dictator who destroyed his own party and betrayed the hopes of a land fit for heroes. In the 1930s he was mistrusted for his admiration of Adolf Hitler and in 1940 many suspected that he would negotiate peace with Hitler if Churchill lost the war. But the judgement of

historians today is unequivocal. In 1999 a millennium poll of historians placed Lloyd George as second only to Churchill as the outstanding prime minister of the 20th century. The historian A J P Taylor went further, calling him the greatest leader since Oliver Cromwell. Arguably, Winston Churchill was a greater war leader but Lloyd George changed society and the lives of ordinary Britons more than any other prime minister. Both were men of genius and Lloyd George knew what that meant because, never low on self esteem, he regarded himself as one; *The chief difference between ordinary and extraordinary men is that when an extraordinary man is faced by a novel and difficult situation, he extricates himself by adopting a plan which is at once daring and unexpected. That is the mark of genius in a man of action.*

Lord Beaverbrook, who knew both Churchill and Lloyd George, said that 'Churchill was perhaps the greater man. But George was more fun'. Fun he certainly was, with his lack of pomposity, his wit and his optimism revived when it flagged by a bout of hymn-singing in Welsh. In fact his optimism, even in the darkest days of war, must have been extraordinarily inspiring. 'To Lloyd George,' said a family friend, 'every morning was not a new day, but a new life and a new chance.' His personality was magnetic and usually irresistible. 'How can I convey to the reader any just impression of this extraordinary man?' asked John Maynard Keynes. 'He lives and feeds on his immediate surroundings; he is an instrument and a player at the same time; he is a prism, which collects light and distorts it and is most brilliant if the light comes from many quarters at once; a vampire and a medium in one.'[1] This is heady stuff and Frances Stevenson, who met him as an impressionable young woman in 1911, is equal to it. She heard Lloyd George, then Chancellor of the Exchequer, preach in a Welsh chapel near Oxford Circus:

'I instantly fell under the sway of his electric personality. I observed his mastery over his audience. He seemed to establish a personal relationship immediately with every member of it and drew us into his orbit.' Soon after she became governess to his youngest daughter and met him again in Downing Street: 'His eyes scrutinised yours, convinced you they understood all the workings of your heart and mind. But what distinguished him from all other men was a magnetism which made my heart leap, swept aside my judgement, producing an excitement which seemed to permeate my entire being.'[2] She is writing as Lloyd George's lover, which she soon became, but chance acquaintances were equally affected. Many years later, in 1938, the writer C P Snow happened to spend Christmas with Lloyd George at a hotel in Cannes: 'His eyes flashed and sparkled. They were deep blue. In any party they did not leave a single person unnoticed. I kept finding them upon me. They were mischievous, they were clairvoyant, they were often lit up with dashing malice. They were the eyes of one aware, without strain or effort, of any shade or feeling near him.'[3] Siren, Svengali, Welsh Wizard – Lloyd George was called all three. His extraordinary empathy accounted in part for his huge popularity with

> **Frances Stevenson** (1888–1972). The daughter of a religious Scottish farmer and the child of a Genoese artist, she inherited both puritan and bohemian characteristics. She fell in love with David Lloyd George in 1911 when she was employed as governess to his daughter Megan and married him in 1943, after the death of his wife. For 30 years she was content to serve as assistant and mistress, avoiding scandal but antagonising both families. She proved more than competent in both roles, administering his paperwork and the home they chose together at Churt in Surrey. Their daughter, Jennifer, was born in 1929.

the voters but also his reputation as a trickster, particularly among the reserved English establishment with whom he worked. Field Marshal Haig expressed exactly the mistrust and condescension of his class when he commented after a walk with 'Ll-G' in Paris in 1917: 'Quite a pleasant little man when one had him alone, but I should think most unreliable.' Lloyd George's inability to charm the generals in the First World War was a rare but very costly failure.

Part One

THE LIFE

Chapter 1: The Boy David (1863–1905)

David George was born at Chorlton-upon-Medlock near Manchester on 17 January 1863. His father, William, was a schoolmaster and his mother, Elizabeth, the daughter of a shoemaker and Baptist pastor at Llanystumdwy near Caernarvon in North Wales. The year after his birth his father died and his mother took her young family, Mary Ellen, David and William (born after his father's death) to be brought up by her unmarried brother Richard who was following in his father's footsteps at Llanystumdwy. Richard Lloyd moulded David George. He gave him his name (denied to his younger brother who remained all his life William George), guided his steps into the law and politics and remained in constant contact with his nephew until his death in 1917. By that time David Lloyd George was Prime Minister.

Lloyd George said *I do not believe in aristocracy, but I do believe in stock*, and the Lloyds of Llanystumdwy were of good Welsh stock, defined as a mixture of race, religion, language and education. Richard Lloyd was a master-craftsman with a shoe workshop. He was also an auto-didact whose light burned long into the night as he sought self-improvement. He ran the local debating society (the 'village parliament') and regarded politics as a public service to improve people's lives. To this end it was his preferred career for his nephew. Above the hearth he hung a portrait of Abraham Lincoln,

who was assassinated soon after the George family moved in, and the example of the country lawyer who rose to become President of the United States was not lost on David. Politics meant essentially Welsh politics and while this obviously had a political prescription it also meant loyalty to the Welsh national spirit, to the concept of the *Gwerin*, a community of equals owing allegiance to God, the beauty of the Welsh language and culture, and truth.

Richard Lloyd's life centred two miles to the east of Llanystumdwy on the Baptist chapel at Criccieth. Here he was unpaid pastor, practising in his public life as well in as his private the gospel of Christ. He was a famed preacher in the current Welsh style, beginning in very quiet tones but working himself up to a trance-like state of inspiration and ecstasy known as *hwyl,* after which the congregation left chapel dazed and excited. Down from the pulpit he was surprisingly mild and uncensorious. He appeared unconcerned, for example, when young David, aged 11, told him he had lost his faith. On more mature reflection Lloyd George said he had *a religious temperament* but could not accept divine authority. He regarded Jesus Christ as a social reformer rather than a personal redeemer, though he never lost his love of a good sermon or a rousing hymn. At the grimmest time of the Great War he took time off from running the country to prepare a book of his favourite Welsh hymns.

Religion was the vital force in the Welsh revival of the 19th century. Village life revolved round the chapel and its preacher. 'In the pulpit,' wrote a native of Criccieth, 'the artistic soul of Wales found its full and, indeed, about its only expression.' Religion was the inspiration for Welsh poetry and music, particularly the hymn, sung unctuously by an increasing number of choirs. The chapel was also the centre of political dissent for while Welsh Christianity was overwhelmingly Nonconformist, the Church of England possessed the temporal power. All four Welsh dioceses belonged to the Province of Canterbury and no Welsh speaker had been appointed to a Welsh diocese for the last century. According to Lloyd George, speaking in a Parliamentary debate in 1902, there were 12,000 Anglican (Church of England) schools in Wales but half the children attending them (one million) were Nonconformists. At the age of 12 he staged his own protest. When diocesan representatives arrived at his Anglican school at Llanystumdwy on their annual visit to hear the children recite the creed they were met with a wall of silence. Eventually brother William broke it with 'I believe' and the others joined in. David thrashed him as a strike-breaker. Pupil-teachers, a prized way of starting a career, had to be Anglican and had that not been the case at Llanystumdwy then the career of the Boy David, as he was soon to be called, might have been very different. Welsh Nonconformist farmers paid Anglican church tithes and often worked for absentee Anglican landlords. Opposition to the Anglican ascendancy, both squirearchy and clergy, was mobilised in the Dissenting chapels.

'*Beth fydd y bachgen yn hwn*' – 'What shall this child be? – asked Uncle Lloyd, and the answer was a lawyer. David had already excelled in debate in the 'village parliament' and the skills of advocacy were not far removed from preaching or politics. If the law was good enough for Abraham Lincoln then it was good enough for David Lloyd George. So in July 1878 he became an articled clerk for the solicitor's practice of Breese, Jones and Casson in Portmadoc and it was not insignificant that Edward Breeze was the local Liberal agent. In 1882 he qualified as a solicitor and set up his own practice at Criccieth with the customary brass plate: 'D. Lloyd George, Solicitor.' Such was the influence of Uncle Lloyd that his nephew became known locally as 'the young solicitor and Baptist temperance preacher'. 'O, my own dear boy spoke well. Never more striking and effective. Thy protection over him, O Lord' enthused his admiring uncle after one of David's sermons.

Politics was clearly the Boy David's goal. At the age of 18 he visited the House of Commons and noted in his diary: *I will not say but that I eyed the assembly in a spirit similar to that in which William the Conqueror eyed England on his visit to Edward the Confessor, as the region of his future domain. Oh, vanity!*[1]. He made his first political speech four years later, proposing a Land League, as in Ireland, for the protection of Welsh farmers and sat down amid deafening applause. It was in the courtroom, however, that he was best able to fight for Welsh causes and attract publicity for doing so. A famous example was the Llanfrothen burial case, a *cause célèbre*, in which he became a household name for success-fully defending Nonconformists who had the temerity to bury their dead in the local, Anglican, churchyard. Temper-ance, land reform and church disestablishment; already the ambitious young lawyer identified himself with the Welsh causes of the day that had brought about the 'flowing tide' of popular support for Gladstone's Liberal Party. He was shortly to add a fourth – home rule for Wales.

'Beth fydd y bachgen yn hwn'
– 'What shall this child be?'

RICHARD LLOYD

In 1887 D R Daniel, who became a friend of Lloyd George and a well-known trade unionist, met him for the first time: 'He was a young boyish man, in simple clothes. I remember his attractive smile and the incomparable brilliance of his lively blue eyes. I saw in G. something I had not found in any other young Welshmen on the crest of political promise. He seemed nimbler in his mind and bearing, more daring in his views, more heroic in his look, though he smiled most of the time.'[2] Two years before, David Lloyd George had met Margaret (Maggie) Owen of Mynydd Ednyfed, the daughter of a prosperous Methodist farmer. She was a jolly, slightly plump 21-year-old, *a sensible girl without any fuss or affectation*, he wrote. He wooed her through the family servant in his irresistible way: *Now be sensible, Margiad. Just do me the favour of telling Maggie Owen that I can kiss better than those Calvinist louts. Tell her you know because I've tried it out on you!*[3] They married in 1888 despite the opposition of her father and, although they lived more apart than together for most of their marriage, they loved each other until death.

This statement would be less remarkable were it not for the well-known and deserved reputation of Lloyd George for promiscuity. *Love is all right,* he said once, *if you lose no time.* Not for nothing was his nickname 'the Goat'. He had a high sex drive without the furtiveness that often goes with it. Although he knew that the *fast life*, as he called it, could ruin his career he took extraordinary risks. Only two years after his marriage he had an affair with an attractive widow of Caernavon, Mrs Jones, with whom he sang duets in the local drama society. She gave birth to a son who grew up to look remarkably like Richard, Lloyd George's legitimate son who was born the previous year. According to Richard, writing many years later, she was bought off from identifying the boy's father with a large annuity. More infidelities came in quick succession. In the early 1890s he took up with the wife of a Welsh draper, Mrs Timothy Davies, in whose London home he lodged for a while. More scandalous was the confession, in 1896, of Mrs Catherine Edwards of Montgomeryshire that David Lloyd George was the father of her child. Although she subsequently withdrew the confession and a much-publicised divorce case eventually absolved

him of paternity, the rumours remained. Love did not come into it with Lloyd George, apart from Maggie. There was one exception, Frances Stevenson, with whom he began an affair in 1912. They lived together in a bigamous relationship (not in the legal sense) for 27 years and were the parents of a daughter, Jennifer. Considering he was Prime Minister for some of this time it speaks well for the discretion of the age and the remarkable *insouciance* of Lloyd George himself. They married when he was 80 after Maggie's death in 1941.

His first love was politics. He wrote to Maggie before their marriage: *my supreme idea is to get on. To this idea I shall sacrifice everything – except, I trust, honesty. I am prepared to thrust even love itself under the wheels of my Juggernaut if it obstructs the way.*[4] He was elected Liberal MP for Caernavon Boroughs at a by-election in 1890 by the narrow margin of 18 votes. He now moved to London, living in a succession of digs because Maggie was busy bearing his children (Richard in 1889, Mair in 1890, Olwen in 1892, Gwilym in 1894 and later Megan in 1902) and could not bring herself to leave North Wales. He rarely returned for long periods even in the parliamentary recess, partly because MPs were unpaid and he was busy stumping the country speaking for £5 a time several nights a week. This footloose life undoubtedly caused strain in the marriage; perhaps Maggie recalled his analogy of the Juggernaut.

> *My supreme idea is to get on. To this idea I shall sacrifice everything – except, I trust, honesty.*
>
> LLOYD GEORGE

As a Member of Parliament David Lloyd George concentrated on Welsh affairs. He knew where his support came from and he did not want to disappoint, writing to D R Daniel: *I never had a hand stretched to me from above, but I've had hundreds of zealous and faithful friends pushing me from behind.* Fully five times as many voters in Wales supported Gladstone's Liberal Party as any other. How sincere Lloyd George was espousing Welsh causes is open to doubt. Certainly he tired of Nonconformism and the interminable debates over church disestablishment. When Maggie remonstrated with him for not going to chapel on a Sunday in London he complained about *being cramped up in a suffocating, malodorous chapel listening to some superstitious rot.*

He was an opportunist over his new cause of home rule for Wales. He caught the tide of resentment against the English, at least in North Wales, and sailed on it with a strong wind: *England has treated with contempt the sacrifice of loyalty rendered by little Wales – it has accorded her grievances nothing but cold neglect – it has lavished upon her pet institutions unmitigated derision; the prospect of Wales would be brighter if her destinies were controlled by a people whose forefathers proved their devotion on a thousand battlefields with their hearts' blood ...* and so on.[5] In 1895 he seconded a motion in Parliament for 'local legislative assemblies' for Ireland, Scotland and Wales. He became a leading speaker for *Cymru Fydd* ('Wales of the Future') an association pushing for self-government. It failed through lack of enthusiasm among the mercantile classes of Cardiff, Swansea and Newport, towns in South Wales with increasing non-

Lady Megan Lloyd George of Dwfor (1902–66). The younger daughter of David Lloyd George, she was born in Criccieth in 1902. She was elected Liberal MP for Anglesey in 1929 and followed her father into the Independent Liberal Party between 1931 and 1945. Defeated in the election of 1951, in 1955 she joined the Labour Party and became MP for Carmarthen in 1957. She was first and foremost a Welsh radical and lived in Criccieth, unmarried, for much of her life. She was devoted to her father's politics but never forgave Frances Stevenson, her former governess, for her long-standing affair with him.

Welsh populations that looked towards England. In fact he took an inclusive view of home rule, following the Chamberlain slogan of 'Home Rule All Round', meaning a partial autonomy within the British Empire for all those who wanted it. Indeed, he admired Joseph Chamberlain who split with the Liberal Party because of his disapproval of complete Home Rule for Ireland, more than he liked William Gladstone who resigned as Prime Minister in 1894 because he could not obtain Home Rule: *I did not like him much. He hated Nonconformists and had no real sympathy with the working classes*, said Ll-G. As far as home rule for Wales was concerned his peroration was stronger than his political conviction.

This was not true of his support for the Boers in the South African War. From the start in 1899 he sympathised with the Boers, seeing them as a pastoral community like Welshmen before the industrial revolution. More than that: *These men are God-fearing men; they are the kind of men who are a simple type of the old Welsh Covenanters*. He supported their claim for independence under his slogan 'Home Rule All Round', assuming it would lead to a free association within the British Empire. He feared, rightly, that they would only be subdued after much suffering, cruelty and cost. Lloyd George opposed the war bravely, for war fever consumed England, if not Wales. On one occasion he won over a hostile audience with his quick-witted repartee: 'Home rule for hell' interrupted a heckler. *Quite right*, retorted Ll-G, *let every man speak up for his own country*. But on 18 December 1901 he addressed a mob of 7,000 flag-waving, whistle-blowing, chanting and stamping interrupters in Birmingham Town Hall and was lucky to escape unharmed. He tried his best as an opening line – *this is a rather lively meeting for a peace meeting* – but he did not get much further. He escaped disguised as a policeman. In the pitched battle that followed one policeman and one rioter were killed, at least 40 injured and the Town Hall wrecked.

Lloyd George was no narrow Welsh nationalist. Although still a backbencher he moved on the national stage. Even on Welsh issues he mixed with the big players in London: newspaper proprietors not local journalists; bishops not parish priests; Liberal Party bigwigs not election agents. Nevertheless he was extraordinarily popular in Wales, largely because of his platform performances in an age of mass

I pause. I reach out my hand to the people and draw them to me. Like children they seem then. Like little children.

LLOYD GEORGE

meetings. 'At Bangor the whole meeting rose to its feet and met him with acclamation. Here he was before his own people, laughing with them, moving them to pathos and pity. He is among his own family; the laugh is the laugh of love, and their very eyes are full of affection as they watch him.'[6] And again: 'When he spoke, the wonderful voice, every note of it under absolute control, would cause thrills to pass through those who listened, making them laugh and cry alternately, and always ending by rousing them in a frenzy of enthusiasm.'[7] Lloyd George manipulated his audience like an actor or, to use his own comparison, like a schoolteacher: *I pause. I reach out my hand to the people and draw them to me. Like children they seem then. Like little children.* The Boy David was a star performer in Parliament as well as in public. Through his opposition to the Boer War he was the best-known radical politician in the country. After ten years of Conservative and Unionist government (1895–1905) the country wanted a change and waited with fascination to see what preferment awaited him. In anticipation, he ceased to practice as a solicitor and handed over the firm to his brother William, who for some years had done most of the work and helped pay for his brother's career.

Chapter 2: The People's David (1905–16)

Lloyd George was on holiday in Italy when he was summoned back by the new Liberal Prime Minister, the elderly Sir Henry Campbell-Bannerman, to be in the Cabinet as President of the Board of Trade. His style of work quickly became clear. He hated to read official boxes of papers and disliked office routine. He also hated reading, never mind answering, correspondence from his constituents. He would stuff letters into his pockets or leave them piling up on his doormat before a casual clearout. 'He likes people to come and talk,' wrote one of his officials. 'He also possesses a great gift of imposing on people the idea that he sees, while agreeing with their side of the question, to the exclusion of all other aspects'. This was negotiation of a high order. Although Ll-G always saw the other point of view he was determined to stick to his essential argument and drive it through; he combined patience and understanding with urgency and single-mindedness.

As President of the Board of Trade he hosted many meetings of businessmen, industrialists and trade unionists. After tough negotiation there emerged the Merchant Shipping Act (1906), the Patents Act (1907) and the Port of London Authority Act (1908). His settling of a national rail strike in 1907 showed his extraordinary skill as a conciliator, as here described by his Junior Minister Lord Devonport: 'They condescended to come (seventeen chairmen and twelve managers of railway companies) and when he began they were frigid, indifferent, barely attentive. I could see their little smiles and nudges with which they punctuated his opening sentences. Then came a change. Within a few minutes every man in his audience was following the speaker with rapt attention. When he ceased speaking the whole situation had altered. Never have I seen a projection of personality so rapid, so completely triumphant. They were almost meek. They were willing there and then to accept his proposals leading to a settlement.'[1] This reads like a description of stage hypnosis. In fact, in the first place, it was the result of Lloyd George's courage (and optimism) to face his adversaries; then his magnetism of voice and eye directed at an audience that he intuitively understood, and then his powers as a speaker. He flattered, he sought common ground, he appeared completely open and ready to compromise, but he was thoroughly briefed and knew exactly how much of his argument he needed to keep, even if he disguised it.

No one would say that David Lloyd George spoke the truth, the whole truth and nothing but the truth. What politician does? Undoubtedly he was carried away at times with his glibness and then protested too much in order to justify it. An example was his appointment as Chancellor of the Exchequer by the new Prime Minister Herbert Asquith in April 1908, after Campbell-Bannerman had resigned through ill health. Lloyd George passed the news of his appointment to the editor of the *Daily Chronicle* in strictest confidence. Not surprisingly the editor printed it and Ll-G was accused of leaking the information. He wrote to Asquith in righteous indignation: *I ought to know who it is among my colleagues who deems me capable of what is not only a gross indiscretion but a downright and discreditable breach of trust.* In the same way might a young woman protest her innocence after inviting her boyfriend into her bedroom and being seduced. Much

more serious was the Marconi scandal in 1912 which showed Ll-G's sly reliance on semantics to get him out of a spot. He and the Attorney General, Sir Rufus Isaacs, bought shares in the American Marconi Company from Isaac's brother, just when the British Marconi Company was about to enter a profitable deal with the government to build six long-range radio stations across the Empire. It looked like a major case of sleaze by the government ministers most involved. They protested their innocence in the House of Commons by denying they had made 'one single transaction with the shares of that company'. The Attorney General implied by 'that company' the British Marconi Company, but this was a case of being economical with the truth if ever there was one. Lloyd George offered to resign and Asquith told the King, George V, that his behaviour had been 'lamentable'. Eventually a Parliamentary inquiry exonerated them but the mud stuck; more evidence for those who wanted it that 'the little Welsh attorney', as opponents called him with a sneer, was a trickster.

By now his appearance had changed from that of the ascetic, pale-faced young man to the plumpish, sleek look of his middle years. His eyes were no longer described as 'burning' but 'twinkling'. His unkempt brown hair down to his collar and full moustache gave him a kind but roguish look. His appearance no doubt affected his reputation. Was he dishonest about money? He had little financial inheritance and now he enjoyed an expensive though homely lifestyle. Unintimidated by the archaic and snobbish trappings of the aristocracy – *I detest court life*, he wrote to Maggie, *the whole atmosphere reeks with Toryism* – he preferred the company of the self-made *nouveaux riches* who lived in the Home Counties, played golf, drove cars and holidayed on the French and Italian rivieras. They enjoyed money and were casual about how they acquired it. Lloyd George was too, with the added justification in his own eyes that he had no time to earn money because he was wholly taken up with politics. He needed to accept gifts and speculate on the markets. This did not make him dishonest necessarily but neither was he a beacon of financial probity. He tended to shove cheques casually into his pockets like he did the letters of constituents, forgetting how they got there and whether they needed justifying.

When the Liberal government of 1905 had been voted in with a huge majority David Lloyd George had warned his party: *If at the end of an average term of office it were found that the present Parliament had done nothing to cope seriously with the social condition of the people, to remove the national degradation of slums and widespread poverty and destitution in a land glittering with wealth, if they do not provide an honourable sustenance for deserving old age, if they tamely allow the House of Lords to extract all virtue out of their bills, so that when the Liberal statute book is produced it is simply a bundle of sapless legislative faggots fit only for the fire – then a new cry will arise for a land with a new party, and many of us will join in that cry.*[2] He was looking over his shoulder at the rising Labour Party that had just won 30 seats in the House of Commons only five years after its foundation. Initially the Libs and Labs had worked together but a story of these years is that of the Liberal Party, led by the 'People's David', forcing through radically reforming welfare legislation to keep at bay a Labour Party that was emerging remorselessly as the party of the newly-empowered working class. The result was a transformed Liberalism that brought in the most profound social reforms until the welfare state of Beveridge and the Labour Government of 1945. This necessitated a major constitutional change to the House of Lords and provoked well over two years of political crisis (1909–11), way beyond normal party strife. Only Lloyd George could have succeeded.

LLOYD THE LUBRICATOR.

His appointment as Chancellor was an act of faith more than reason on Asquith's part because Ll-G had neither a business nor a financial background. In fact he held the post for seven years, the longest period of occupancy between Pitt the Younger and Gordon Brown. His ally, and successor at the Board of Trade, was Winston Churchill who was similarly impatient with the old Liberalism and equally single-minded. Churchill was Ll-G's only rival as speechmaker and opportunist. They were a formidable combination with Ll-G as the senior partner. Over a decade later, in 1924 when Churchill was Chancellor of the Exchequer, he called on Lloyd George for advice. 'Within five minutes,' he told a friend afterwards, 'the old relationship was completely re-established. The relationship between master and servant, and I was the servant'.

A simple prelude, as it were, was the passing of the Old Age Pensions Bill of 1908. It promised five shillings a week paid for by the Treasury to individuals over 70 who were neither receiving poor relief nor earning more than £26 a year (£39 for couples). It only affected just over half a million pensioners, an interesting fact about the demography of the time.

> *'Within five minutes, the old relationship was completely re-established. The relationship between master and servant, and I was the servant.'*
>
> WINSTON CHURCHILL

The keystone of the Lloyd George social programme was the so-called 'People's Budget' of 1909. For the first time taxation was fully acknowledged as a major instrument of social reform, for the rich were to be taxed – super-taxed – for the benefit of the poor. Ll-G's budget speech was, according to the Liberal backbencher Hilaire Belloc, 'without exception the worst speech that has been delivered in the House of Commons'. This cannot be true but for once he did perform badly. All too conscious of the momentous occasion, for the substance of his budget required a four-hour exposition, he plodded through endless typewritten notes in a voice dulled by tiredness and a throat infection. He said afterwards that he had not been aiming at *hwyl* but setting down his manifesto. In any event his reasoning was lucid. In order to pay for a huge deficit caused by rearmament and old age pensions he intended to increase income tax, introduce super-tax of 6d in the pound for those earning more than £5,000 p.a., charge publicans more for their licences and drinkers more for their spirits and tobacco. Finally he intended to impose three land taxes, one of them a capital gains tax on the 'unearned increment' of land enhanced in value by the efforts of those who worked on it. He then outlined his schemes for social reform, namely his proposals for sickness and unemployment insurance.

It was the proposals for land taxes that most enraged his opponents, particularly in the House of Lords, and this was an issue that Lloyd George felt strongly about all his life (see later). He now issued a threat: *There are hundreds of thousands of Liberals who will say that if the land proposals are abandoned then the party is perfectly hopeless as an effective machine and it is high time to form or federate with another.* To add to the sense of crisis, the previous Liberal Prime Minister Lord Rosebery put forward a sweeping criticism of the budget that carried great resonance: 'It is not a Budget, but a revolution. It will be carried over the heads of the people without the faintest desire to ascertain their views.' The House of Lords refused to pass the budget, the first time it had interfered with a financial bill since the 17th century, and thereby forced a general election. *The great assize of the people* (in Lloyd George's words) would decide.

The constitutional struggle of Peers versus People now began. Much to the surprise of Lloyd George, the general

THE CHANCE OF A LIFETIME.

Our Mr. Asquith. "Five hundred coronets, dirt-cheap! This line of goods ought to make business a bit brisker, what?"

Our Mr. Lloyd George. "Not half; bound to go like hot cakes."

[December 28, 1910.]

election of February 1910 resulted in only a tiny majority of Liberals over Conservatives of just two seats. In the circumstances King Edward VII refused to create more Liberal peers as a ploy to get the budget through the House of Lords, at least not until another general election. Whether the Liberal Cabinet originally intended to by-pass the House of Lords veto by this ploy or intended from the beginning to use the budget as a cudgel to crush its right of veto has divided historians. Lloyd George certainly made clear his dislike of the House of Lords in provocative terms. *It is no more than five hundred ordinary men chosen at random from amongst the unemployed*, he announced in one speech that particularly annoyed Edward VII. In any event, now there was little option; either lose the 'People's Budget', or at least further reforming legislation, or pass a Parliament Bill to reduce the power of the House of Lords.

It [the House of Lords] *is no more than five hundred ordinary men chosen at random from amongst the unemployed.*

LLOYD GEORGE

In April 1910 the Parliament Bill passed its first reading in the House of Commons. It removed any control over financial legislation from the House of Lords and downgraded its veto on other legislation to delaying powers that could only be used twice on the same bill in the life of a parliament. A few days later the 'people's budget' also sailed through the Commons and the Lords, preferring to hold their fire for constitutional warfare, passed it too. A month later Edward VII died and wags said the two events were not unconnected. With the constitutional weapon at the ready Prime Minister Asquith needed the country's approval before he wielded it. The Liberals called for and won another general election in December 1910. The result was a tie with the Conservatives (272 seats each) so that they had to rely on the support of

Labour and Irish MPs to allow them to govern. In March 1911 the Parliament Bill passed its second reading in the House of Commons and reached the House of Lords. George V threatened the Lords with the creation of more Liberal peers if it vetoed it (the rumour was that the new king had promised Asquith he would do so before he called the general election). This was too much for their Lordships in the opposition, both the 'Ditchers' and the 'Hedgers' (those determined to die in the last ditch and those anxious to find a way round the hedge above it) and the Bill became an Act in August 1911. But the bitter confrontation set the tone of British politics for many years.

'I like Lloyd George', said the new leader of the Conservative Party Andrew Bonar Law. 'He is a nice man, but the most dangerous little man that ever lived.' The man concerned wrote a revealing reply to a fan letter from the Prime Minister's daughter: *We ought to thank God that Labour had no daring leader otherwise British Liberalism could have become what Continental Liberalism is now – a respectable middle class affair – futile and impotent.* He knew that the fortunes of his party depended on the fortunes of another – Labour. Determined to keep the working class vote Lloyd George now pressed on with his National Insurance Bill, Part I (sickness) and Part II (unemployment).

'I like Lloyd George. He is a nice man, but the most dangerous little man that ever lived'.

BONAR LAW

The only redress available to the poor working man and woman who became ill was a Poor Law hospital and charitable dispensary. Those better off, the so-called 'aristocrats of labour', contributed insurance money to Friendly Societies like the Hearts of Oak or to their trade unions, but this was frequently insufficient to cover anything but a decent funeral;

Lloyd George and the Office of Prime Minister

'Lloyd George's regime as wartime prime minister was without precedent. It marked a political and constitutional revolution as a new leviathan of state power was created. The controversy surrounding his role in Downing Street concerned mainly the nature of his authority. He seemed to be turning the premiership into something like the American presidency ... He created at once a supreme war cabinet of five men to run the war. The traditional cabinet system seemed to be dissolving.

The centralisation of wartime government and the personal ascendancy of the premier were underpinned by two further innovations. The Cabinet Office, under Sir Maurice Hankey, became a formidable machine of government, extending the control of the prime minister to all departments, civilian and military. There was yet another novelty, the prime minister's own secretariat at Downing Street, popularly called the "Garden Suburb" because it first met in huts in the gardens of no.10. These personal advisers underlined how presidential the traditional system of British cabinet government was becoming. The entire atmosphere seemed to many alarming, even sinister. But a war had to be won, and perhaps it was no time for constitutional niceties.

Lloyd George was the most powerful prime minister since the younger Pitt, perhaps ever ... The constitution seemed to be cast aside by a presidential prime minister backed up by his Cabinet Office while the cabinet itself dissolved into *ad hoc* "conferences of ministers". The "Garden Suburb" aroused particular hostility. Even more did the activity of Sir William Sutherland in undercover deals with the press and in the trafficking of titles and honours in return for contributions to government or party funds. Critics quoted Dunning's famous resolution against Lord North's government in 1780 that the power of the prime minister had increased, was increasing and ought to be diminished.'

[George, Lloyd David in the *Dictionary of National Biography* by Kenneth O Morgan, pp 899–900, 903.]

a case of too little too late. Part I of the new bill required all workers between 16 and 60 earning less than £160 p.a. to insure themselves with these approved Societies, according to Ll-G's irresistible formula of '9d for 4d'; the worker paid 4d, the employer 2d and the government 3d. Each worker would be issued with a card filled in by the employer with stamps purchased from the post office. Sickness, disability, maternity, sanatorium and medical benefits would follow. Those earning above the rate could join provided they paid the employer's contribution too. The same principle applied to Part II, the unemployment benefit. Both employee and employer were to contribute 2.5d per week to which the state would add 1d. The benefit would apply for 15 weeks at 7 shillings per week. At first this benefit would only apply compulsorily to half a dozen industries where labour fluctuated heavily, such as building, shipbuilding and iron-founding. Part I of the scheme was to be run through the Friendly Societies and the British Medical Association; Part II through the new labour exchanges working with trade unions. The Bill was received with great enthusiasm on all sides of the House of Commons – but then negotiations began.

Once again, only Lloyd George could have pulled it off. In the Commons he always appeared in charge whatever the mood of the House and however difficult the subject matter. A civil servant recalled 'Lloyd George rising to reply, knowing practically nothing about the particular facts, briefed as he went along by little scraps of paper passed along the bench from the officials' boxes, and yet leaving the impression that he had a more complete mastery of every detail than his critic.' Outside the debating chamber he received dozens of delegations, displaying a sweet temper or a brutal manner according to requirements. He changed tack adroitly; he scattered about promises; he produced a concession as if it had just come to hand when, in fact, it had been up his sleeve for weeks; he stumped the country. He wore himself out and reduced at least two civil servants to nervous breakdowns. The Bill reached the Statute Book in December 1911 and Winston Churchill declared with pride: 'We are an insured nation. This tremendous step can never be retracted. You and your children and your children's children will be influenced by this legislation every week of their lives.'[3]

Beatrice Webb, one of the founding intellectuals of the Labour Party, wrote peevishly in her diary: 'Lloyd George and Winston Churchill have taken the *limelight* not only from their colleagues but from the Labour Party. They stand out as the most advanced politicians … The splendid reception given to Lloyd George's sickness insurance is a curious testimony to the heroic demagogy of the man.'[4]

In fact, although he relished the party victory, Lloyd George was not at heart a party politician. He was more a dynamic man of action than a party advocate. Skilled though he was in arguing proposed legislation back and forth across the Commons like counsel in a law court, what he wanted most was to get things done. His frustration had surfaced the previous summer, in between the two general elections, when he had issued an extraordinary Memorandum on the Formation of a Coalition: *This country has gained a good deal from the conflict and rivalry of the parties; but I cannot help thinking that the time has come for a truce, for bringing the resources of the two parties into a joint stock in order to liquidate arrears which, if much longer neglected, may end in national impoverishment, if not insolvency.*[5] His suggestion was that most of the supposedly controversial issues of the day – Free Trade, Lords' reform, Irish Home Rule, Welsh disestablishment – were in fact not controversial and could be settled by independent commissions. With these time-consuming issues delegated elsewhere,

a new national administration could focus on the crucial needs of the day like social reform and national defence. This bombshell, striking as it did the core of parliamentary politics, was far too radical to get anywhere, though fellow free spirits like Churchill were excited by it. The significance of the Memorandum is that it showed Lloyd George's preference for strong executive government. In six years time, as wartime Prime Minister, he would rule in this way. But his continued preference in the 1920s, when dictatorial governments were rising left and right, tainted his reputation as a democrat.

In the eyes of the suffragettes a more immediate blemish was Lloyd George's handling of votes for women. He claimed to be a suffragist, unlike Prime Minister Asquith who agreed with Gladstone that 'the natural sphere (of women) was not the turmoil and dust of politics, but the circle of social and domestic life'. Nevertheless, he spoke against a private member's bill, the Conciliation Bill, which would have allowed limited franchise for women because he argued that most of the new women voters would be Conservative. What he wanted was overall electoral reform that would end, too, the denial of the vote to 40 per cent of adult males. It was a matter of principle as well as politics but the fiery suffragette champion Christabel Pankhurst did not see it that way. According to the editor of *The Manchester Guardian*, C P Scott, who was a friend and informant of Ll-G: 'She envisages the whole suffragette movement as a gigantic duel between herself and Lloyd George whom she designed to destroy.' She nearly succeeded. Once again, as during the Boer War, his speeches were interrupted and even broken up. His new house at Walton Heath was actually blown up by a suffragette bomb. In 1912 a government bill on the Lloyd George lines was introduced to Parliament but withdrawn on a technicality; then the World War intervened. Women had to wait until 1918 for the vote and then it was given only to those who were 30 and over. Had Lloyd George shown the same range of skills and the same determination that had put more complex social reforms on the statute books, then women's suffrage could have been added to the list of Liberal successes at least four years earlier. It was, for once, a failure of resolve but not a failure of intention.

Unlike many of his countrymen, Lloyd George went to war reluctantly in August 1914. He feared the destruction it would cause and he regretted the shelving of further social reforms, but when Germany invaded Belgium he saw that Britain's national security was threatened. In fact once war was declared he immediately appreciated the party truce and relished the firm executive action it encouraged. He calmed the *flapping penguins* in the City by obtaining government promises for the Treasury to underwrite debts caused by the war and to issue new currency notes. He sought to increase war production by limiting the consumption of alcohol during working hours and persuading George V to take the temperance pledge. He negotiated a Treasury Agreement with the Trades Union Congress (TUC) that encouraged women to work in factories and obtained the promise of no strike action in return for vague promises to curtail profiteering.

It was his speech at the Queen's Hall in London on 19 September that made the most impact. Overnight he became the government's spokesman justifying the war in quasi-religious terms; the lay preacher of patriotism: *The stern hand of Fate has scourged us to an elevation where we can see the great everlasting things that matter for a nation – the great peaks we had forgotten, of Honour, Duty, Patriotism, and clad in glittering white, the great pinnacle of Sacrifice pointing like a rugged finger to Heaven. We shall descend into the valleys again; but as long as* the men and women of this generation last, they will carry in their hearts the image of those great mountain peaks whose foundations are not shaken, though Europe rock and sway in the convulsions of a great war.[6]

Both Asquith and Sir Edward Grey, the Foreign Secretary, confessed that they read the speech in tears but there was an element of humbug about it. Only a few weeks before he had written to Maggie *I am not going to sacrifice my nice boy. He [Gwilym] must on no account be bullied into serving abroad.* The speech served its purpose in stirring the nation but the idea that the sacrifice of war atones for the *indulgence and selfishness of peace* made war sound noble and peace almost a sin; a concept that would appeal to the fascists in the next World War. Calling Germany *the road hog of Europe* seems to pass the test of time more easily.

I am not going to sacrifice my nice boy. He [Gwilym] *must on no account be bullied into serving abroad.*

LLOYD GEORGE

In hindsight, Lloyd George's understanding of overall military strategy was far more right than wrong. 'Ll-G,' wrote Churchill, 'has more true insight and courage than anyone else. He really sticks at nothing – no measure is too far reaching, no expedient too novel.' He realised from the end of 1914 that the war on the Western Front was bogged down *in an eternal stalemate*, a war of attrition that was *too horrible to think of.* He was constantly pushing for new initiatives on other foreign fields, either against the Austrians by removing troops from Flanders and opening a front on the Dalmatian Coast or at Salonika (now Thessalonica); or against the Turks by forcing the Dardanelles and taking Istanbul. As he put it in his *War Memoirs*: *We hammered at the breastplate of Achilles and neglected his heel.* Over the Dardanelles he was in agreement with Churchill, but with one major proviso: *if we failed at the Dardanelles we ought to be ready to try something else ... in the Near East. The army would not be required or expected to pull the chestnuts out of the fire for the navy.*[7] This is exactly what happened in the debacle of Gallipoli in the summer of 1915, for which Churchill took the blame. The following spring Lloyd George questioned the plans for the Battle of the Somme, though surprisingly ineffectually, and when that July of 1916 the dreadful attack was launched he did not share Haig's optimism about its result (see later).

It was as Minister of Munitions that Lloyd George saved the British Army from defeat. Field Marshal Lord Horatio Kitchener had been appointed Secretary of State for War in 1914. A victor of small wars he may have been, and an erect bearing with a fine moustache he certainly possessed, but he was out of his depth in an appointment that was as much political as military. Autocratic and uncommunicative, lacking imagination and bogged down in detail, pessimistic and complacent at the same time, he was a disastrous appointment. Lloyd George was infuriated to hear Kitchener announce in early 1915 that it would not be possible to equip new army recruits with rifles until 1916 and horrified when he commented after the defeat at Neuve Chapelle in March 1915 that the loss of soldiers was less serious than the loss of munitions because soldiers were easier to replace. At this time Frances Stevenson, now serving as Lloyd George's secretary, was told that her brother had been killed on the Western Front. 'What he must have suffered, fighting with little ammunition and no explosives, he was never able to tell us, for he was killed in May,' she wrote forlornly.[8] For Lloyd George it was time for executive action. After much political infighting and a threat of resignation he became Minister of Munitions that month and managed to set up his new ministry independent of the War Office. He was helped by a press campaign against Kitchener. 'NEED FOR SHELLS' thundered a *Times* headline. 'BRITISH ATTACK CHECKED; LIMITED SUPPLIES THE CAUSE.' It was a nominal demotion and a career gamble but he soon became a spectacular success.

When Lloyd George and his two assistants (one of them Frances Stevenson) moved into their new base in Whitehall Gardens they found one table and two chairs. By the time he left two years later the staff numbered 12,000. By the end of the war it was up to 65,000 with three million workers under its control. 'The whole island was an arsenal' said his successor Winston Churchill. Ll-G's first task was recruitment; *men of push and go* he was after and it became a catch-phrase that applied more to him than anyone. Civil servants like William Beveridge sat side by side with 'outsiders' like railway magnate Sir Eric Geddes and the shipowner Sir George Booth. Frances Stevenson sent out a questionnaire to 65,000 workshops to compile a massive inventory of the whole industry. By the end of the year the department had built 60 new munitions factories and commandeered over 750 workshops, laboratories and supply depots. It had begun to demand weekly reports giving details of output from which, for example, it calculated that the production of shells had increased from 70,000 per month in May to 120,000 in September to 238,000 by January 1916.

Men of push and go.

LLOYD GEORGE

The Ministry was now responsible for the production of rifles, artillery pieces, machine guns, bombs, trench warfare equipment, military transport, tanks, optical instruments and ammunition. It saw its remit to plan two years ahead with the aim of equipping the army fully for defensive operations by the end of 1915 and offensive operations from March

1916. Lloyd George's mind, as ever, was ranging over new initiatives, particularly weaponry. He pushed the development of the Stokes mortar to counter the German *Minenwerfer* and claimed credit, rightly, for adequately supplying the army with the most decisive weapon of trench warfare, the machine gun. This was despite the opposition of Kitchener. In a famous exchange of estimates, the War Minister said that only four machine guns per battalion were needed; more was luxury. Lloyd George told Geddes, whom he placed in charge of production, *take Kitchener's maximum, square it and multiply that by two; and when you are in sight of that double it again for good luck.* Finally, Lloyd George quickly saw the advantage of the tank or 'landship' as it was called. He personally sanctioned the new tanks that were used in battle for the first time in September 1916.

The Ministry became the largest wartime employer, notably of women who made up half the workforce of the arsenals, an unhealthy and dangerous job. Lloyd George asked his old friend and social reformer Seebohm Rowntree to supervise factory welfare. Before long a factory inspectorate began work, canteens opened, flats and hostels were built for women and boy workers, and wage rates were standardised. Throughout the industry the Munitions of War Act (July 1916) strengthened the Treasury Agreement by forbidding strikes, requiring wage claims to be settled by arbitration and forbidding workers to seek jobs elsewhere; profits were pegged to pre-war levels. In 13 months Lloyd George had changed forever relations between the British state and industry. For the duration of the war the British army was never again short of guns and ammunition.

By mid-1915 it was obvious that Asquith was incapable of being a wartime Prime Minister. Whereas Lloyd George showed a single-minded determination to win the war,

Asquith was indecisive and distracted. His energies were spent handling an increasingly fractious Cabinet, most of the members of which also sat on the daily War Committee, thereby duplicating the time spent in discussion. The MP Leo Amery passed his verdict on Asquith with a memorable metaphor: 'The Supreme power of the State has fallen in to the hands of a man who combines unrivalled gifts of parliamentary leadership with a complete incapacity to face facts or come to any decision on them. For twenty years he has held a season ticket on the line of least resistance, and gone wherever the train of events has carried him, lucidly justifying his position at whatever point he has happened to find himself.'[9] Frances Stevenson observed that his concentration was made worse by the decision of his young *confidante* Venetia Stanley to get married. Asquith would even read and answer her letters during Cabinet meetings, 'then ring for the messenger who would take the reply for despatch'. She added that Ll-G considered Cabinet meetings *a waste of time*.

The first solution was a coalition government and some suggested Lloyd George should lead it. He pleaded his innocence of scheming and Asquith seemed convinced. Nevertheless, the Prime Minister's description of it in a letter to Venetia Stanley revealed a typical Lloyd George performance, protesting his innocence too much: 'His eyes were wet with tears. He declared he would rather (1) break stones, (2) dig potatoes (3) be hanged and quartered than do any act, or say a word, or harbour a thought that was disloyal to me.' The Coalition Government was formed on 25 May 1915 with Asquith still at its head. It is true that Lloyd George made no personal move to seize the premiership. He was more interested in power than office and really wanted a free hand to win the war; but even at the time he was utterly scornful of Asquith's leadership and prepared to undermine it. His famous 'too late' speech in Parliament on 20 December could have brought down the government: *Too late in moving here, too late in coming to this decision, too late in starting with enterprises, too late in preparing! In this war the footsteps of the Allied forces have been dogged by the spectre of 'too late', and unless we quicken our movements, damnation will fall on the sacred cause for which so much gallant blood has flowed.*[10]

In fact the Prime Minister of 'wait and see', as the cartoonists dubbed him, limped on for another year, tired, shaky and dilatory after eight years in office. By the summer of 1916, according to Lloyd George in his *War Memoirs*, the behaviour of Asquith was pitiful: [Asquith] *gave the impression of a man who was overwhelmed, distracted and enfeebled not merely by the weight and complexity of his burdens. Whether he was ever fitted for the position of a War Minister in the greatest struggle in the history of the world may be open to doubt, but that he was quite unfitted at this juncture to undertake so supreme a task was not open to question or challenge. Asquith's will became visibly flabbier, tardier and more flaccid under the strain of war.*[11]

The war went from bad to worse with the failure of the

Field Marshal Sir William Robertson (1860–1933): Born in Welborn, Lincolnshire, he enlisted as a private in the British Army in 1877 and rose to the rank of Field Marshal in 1920, an unprecedented career from bottom to top. Having served with distinction in India, South Africa and Northern France (1914–15) he was appointed Chief of the Imperial General Staff in 1915. Like Haig, whom he always supported, he believed that forces should be concentrated in the primary theatre of war in order to overwhelm the enemy in decisive battle. The results were the Somme and Passchendaele. Lloyd George lost confidence in him and downgraded him in 1918 to Commander-in-Chief, Home Forces.

Somme offensive in July and August. Yet the government seemed to have no option except, in Lloyd George's words, *of repeating the old fatuous tactics of hammering away with human flesh and sinews at the strongest fortresses of the enemy*. In May conscription had been introduced. Lloyd George was all in favour *not in principle but of necessity* but the idea of forcing men to fight went against all Liberal principles and the issue split the party; ever after it was held against Lloyd George as a major betrayal. On 6 June Kitchener had drowned when his ship struck a mine on the way to Russia and for six months Ll-G took over as Minister for War, but the office had been stripped of real meaning. To by-pass Kitchener, Sir William Robertson had been appointed Chief of the Imperial General Staff (CIGS) with effective control of war strategy, in the same way as Lloyd George had effective control of munitions. In November 1916 Robertson made the shrewd observation to a newspaper that in Cabinet and War Council (the new but scarcely smaller War Committee) Asquith behaved more like a judge than president. The only man who could decide quickly 'Yes' or 'No' was Lloyd George.

The life of the country depends on resolute action by you now.

LLOYD GEORGE TO BONAR LAW

Depressed and angered by Asquith's inertia, Lloyd George considered resignation. Then he proposed that Asquith should remain as Prime Minister while he got on with running the war as head of a civilian triumvirate, a War Council of himself, the Conservative Leader Andrew Bonar Law and the Ulster Unionist Sir Edward Carson. Asquith not surprisingly rejected this proposal. The press campaigned to remove Asquith and praised Lloyd George. Ll-G continued to insist that Asquith could remain as Prime Minister provided his War Council had supreme control of war policy, subject to Asquith's permanent right of veto. Asquith continued to resist this loss of face and loss of power. The deadlock was broken when Lloyd George, having taken soundings that over 100 Liberal MPs would support him come what may, stiffened the resolve of his Tory ally with the famous note, *The life of the country depends on resolute action by you now*. They both resigned, thus forcing Asquith to surrender office too. Bonar Law refused to replace him and on 7 December Lloyd George kissed the King's hand in the time-honoured way and became Prime Minister. Like Winston Churchill in 1940 he was undoubtedly the people's choice, but even Lloyd George's self-confidence was not bullet-proof. *I wonder if I can do it?* he said to Frances Stevenson, sitting in the gloomy War Office.

Part Two

THE LEADERSHIP

Chapter 3: The Man who Won the War (1916–18)

On 9 December 1916, Lloyd George wrote to his brother William: *Presided over my first War Cabinet. Found it embarrassing to be addressed as Prime Minister by all the members ... Tell Uncle Lloyd that he is responsible for putting me in this awful job.* The Boy David from the tiny Welsh village was Prime Minister aged 54 – and few expected his government to last more than six weeks. He wrote in his *War Memoirs*: *I surveyed the possibilities. I was assured of the support of under one half of the Liberal Members in the House. Every Conservative Minister in the Government, except Mr Bonar Law and Mr Balfour* [who had been Prime Minister 1902–05] *was hostile. To understand their attitude it was necessary to bear in mind that there had never before been a 'ranker' raised to the premiership. The attitude of Labour was doubtful, but not altogether antagonistic ... The prospect of success was not encouraging.*[1]

Asquith refused to serve under Lloyd George and other Liberal ministers followed his example. They retreated to the political periphery from where their party has never returned; since December 1916 the Liberals have never again been a party of power. So Lloyd George depended on Conservative support, and here his alliance with the big two, Balfour and Bonar Law, was indispensable.

Stanley Baldwin said that Andrew Bonar Law's co-operation

with Lloyd George during the War was 'the most perfect partnership in political history', and Ll-G did not dissent. United by a humble origin and a stern religious upbringing, for Bonar Law's father was a Presbyterian minister in Scotland, they were otherwise opposites. They enjoyed the creative tension when optimist meets pessimist. Most mornings Ll-G would walk next door 'for a smoke after breakfast' and sound out his schemes on his Chancellor of the Exchequer: *He had an incomparable gift of practical criticism*, wrote Ll-G. *His reaction was always to array all the difficulties and obstacles. When he had finished I knew there was nothing more to be said against my plans. Sometimes, when the force of his adverse criticisms was great, I abandoned my project. Other times I went away strengthened in my resolve. 'Well, Bonar, if there is nothing more to be said against my scheme, I mean to put it before the War Cabinet today'. Once I had secured his consent I had no more loyal supporter for my plans. 'There is a lot of trouble ahead!' warned Bonar Law, but he faced it without faltering.*[2]

> **Arthur Henderson** (1863–1935): The illegitimate son of a housemaid, he became a 'born again Christian' and Nonconformist politician. He was the fifth Labour MP to be elected, for Barnard Castle in 1903. Henderson was a moderate politician, anti-Bolshevik and anti-confrontation in industrial relations. Home Secretary in the first Labour Government and Foreign Secretary in the second he made his reputation as a supporter of the League of Nations and world peace, for which he was awarded a Nobel Prize in 1934. The short-term Leader of the Labour Party in 1931, after Ramsay MacDonald formed the National Government, he lost his seat and resigned in 1932.

Bonar Law, the dutiful and diligent master of every brief, shrank from taking decisions that had fateful consequences. Lloyd George, the man of action who relished risk-taking, seemed to take decisions without a qualm after they had passed his deputy's critical judgement. It was Bonar Law who kept Parliament sweet. He sat for hours in the House of Commons while Ll-G avoided it more and more. (Between February 1917 and February 1918 Bonar Law has 37 columns in the Hansard index and Lloyd George only four.) Bonar Law became Chancellor of the Exchequer and Leader of the Commons but more important he was the government's indispensable anchorman; and in these first few months of office it was he who enabled Lloyd George to govern.

He governed through a small War Cabinet of five – as was always his intention – and choosing the five was key to maintaining a three-party coalition government. Apart from Bonar Law as his Deputy, who attended less than the others, Arthur Henderson, Lord George Curzon and Lord Alfred Milner joined him initially and none of them was given other government responsibilities. Henderson was a Labour leader who supported the war unequivocally, unlike Ramsay MacDonald who had been persuaded to line up Labour behind Lloyd George at a vital meeting early in December: 'Lloyd George was exceedingly amiable but excessively indefinite; like a bit of mercury' he reported afterwards. Lord Curzon was a former Viceroy of India and later Ll-G's Foreign Secretary; pompous and vain, he was cruelly mimicked by the Prime Minister who nevertheless respected him for his worldliness: *He has travelled a lot. He is full of knowledge that none of us possess.* Viscount Milner was Ll-G's trump card, winning over the support of the Tory 'die-hards'. A former Commissioner for South Africa, he had been in retirement for a decade but was hugely respected and he did not disappoint: *Milner was much the best all-round brain that the Conservative Party contributed to our Councils,* wrote Ll-G. Over the next year the War Cabinet met over 300 times, that is almost daily, and over the three

years of its life its total membership numbered nine, of whom Lloyd George was one of only two Liberals. The other was Winston Churchill who joined in 1917. A key figure was Sir Maurice Hankey as Secretary.

He compensated for Ll-G's untidy mind and disinclination to read papers by being a master of detail. Daily the minutes were typed up and circulated to the King, the wider Cabinet and Chiefs of Staff – a practice not followed hitherto. No one doubted the dominance of Lloyd George. Although Bonar Law saw his job as 'hanging on to the coat tails of the Little Man and holding him back' there was little evidence that he succeeded.

'Lloyd George was exceedingly amiable but excessively indefinite; like a bit of mercury.'

RAMSEY MACDONALD

Lloyd-George's government through War Cabinet was the apex of a constitutional revolution that provoked a mixture of admiration and suspicion. Beatrice Webb wrote in her diary on 9 December: 'The Ll-G Government announced today is a brilliant improvisation, reactionary in composition and undemocratic in form. For the first time since Cromwell we have a dictatorship by one, or possibly by three, men. We see Labour leaders in open alliance with Tory chieftains, a Cabinet created neither by party organisations nor by the will of the Commons.'[3]

The truth was that Lloyd George turned the premiership into a presidential rather than parliamentary office. His own cabinet office grew larger, extending the control of the Prime Minister to all departments. One member, Thomas Jones, described his colleagues in a memorable phrase as 'fluid persons moving amongst people who matter'. Then there was the Prime Minister's personal secretariat, popularly called the 'Garden Suburb' because initially it was based in huts in the garden of 10 Downing Street. This was a group of Lloyd-

George's own experts drawn from the press, business and academia who advised him more intimately than senior officers of state. He also had his own assistants, of course, a group of some notoriety. Frances Stevenson was a principal secretary as well as his mistress, with whom he lived when possible at Walton Heath, thereby leaving 10 Downing Street an austere state building rather than a home. His press officer was Sir William 'Bronco Bill' Sutherland, an early master of spin-doctoring. His parliamentary go-between was the Liberal Chief Whip, Sir Freddie Guest, a cousin of Churchill's and a seller of political honours. Outsiders resented the whole set-up, regarding the *coterie* as spies and toadies. 'His means of information are varied and go deep into the camp of his opponents' wrote one critic, but with admiration. 'Conversations with press men and critics are brought to him by agents with a footing in both camps. His secret service is well run, like Napoleon's.'[4] Yet there was a war to be won and Lloyd George was the one who could win it. It was no time for constitutional niceties.

> **Sir Alfred Milner** (1854–1925): He was born in Germany, had a brilliant education and made his reputation in South Africa as High Commissioner 1897–1905. Here he developed his philosophy of responsible imperialism, dedicated to economic and social improvement of the colonies. He argued for the Boer war although he also advocated equal treatment of British and Dutch. Lloyd George brought him into the War Cabinet in 1916 because he admired his administrative skills, his beliefs in central planning and strong leadership. He was Lloyd George's indispensable right hand man but retired, tired and disheartened, in 1918.

By December 1916 the War had reached the point of crisis. Sir William Robertson, the CIGS, wrote Ll-G a note that would have unnerved a lesser man: 'We do not yet nearly realise the stupendous task confronting us. We can only expect to just win through and no more and yet things in England are going on much the same today as two years ago.'[5] The immediate crisis was not on the battlefields of France and Belgium but in the seas around Britain for German U-boats were starving the country of food. Twice as many merchant vessels were being sunk as built, over 600,000 tons of shipping in the last four months of 1916 alone, and it was rumoured that the German Admiralty hoped to bring Britain to its knees by the summer of 1917. In his *War Memoirs* Lloyd George pointed out that *the food question ultimately decided the issue of this War. It was directly responsible for the downfall of Russia and it was the element that led to the collapse of Austria and Germany.*[6] He was not to know this when he became Prime Minister, but he was well aware that Britain imported 60 per cent of its food and nearly all its staple food grain and sugar; yet it was 'business as usual' in the High Street. Ll-G was scathing. *A pathetic document*, he called a report from the First Sea Lord, Admiral Jellicoe, to the effect that submarine warfare was very harmful but 'there is no conclusive answer; we must be content with palliation'. *Dismal and obtuse* is how he castigated the Board of Trade's neglect of home food cultivation. Faced by this crisis as soon as he became Prime Minister, Lloyd George 'saved the country; but it was a close run thing', in the words of his biographer John Grigg. How he did it shows the style of his government. It was urgent and ruthless, improvising and interfering at every level.

In the first place, with his own Ministry of Munitions as a prototype, Lloyd George set up new ministries run by non-politicians; men he selected for their *push and go*. He created a Ministry of Shipping by taking the merchant marine away from the Admiralty and giving it to the charge of a Glasgow ship-owner, Sir Joseph Maclay. In charge of shipbuilding he placed one of his favourite technocrats, Sir Eric Geddes, and before the end of the War 3,000,000 tons of new shipping were built per year. He appointed as President of the Board of Agriculture a former scholar of All Souls and, improbably, a land agent, R E Prothero. They shared a running joke that Ll-G once referred to 'mangel-wurzels produced by pheasants'. Under him there was a new Department of Food Production run by the hugely ambitious Tory MP Arthur Lee. Ll-G was a formidable head-hunter because he relished the company of decisive and argumentative men like himself.

One of his few unsuccessful appointments was the future prime minister Neville Chamberlain, then Mayor of Birmingham. He became Director General of National Service, the new ministry to maximise employment in the war industries. Chamberlain made the mistake of waiting to be told what he was expected to do rather than taking the initiative. Soon, Ll-G's lack of support forced his resignation. He never forgave Lloyd George and the feeling was mutual. Ll-G wrote in *War Memoirs*: *Mr Neville Chamberlain is a man of rigid competency. Such men are indispensable for filling subordinate posts. But they are lost in an emergency or in creative tasks at any time.* And in May 1940, Ll-G had the last word.

In the second place Ll-G's instinct was to sidestep established opinion, especially when it came from the armed forces, by seeking out experts who thought differently. *Much study is a weariness of the flesh*, he wrote in *War Memoirs*, *but conversations with a knowledgeable person stimulate and nourish one's mind.* He was a good listener. On this occasion junior officers and civilians from the new Ministry of Shipping persuaded him that the answer to U-boats was the convoy system whereby Royal Navy destroyers armed with depth charges escorted small fleets of merchantmen. The Board of Admiralty resisted on the grounds that collecting together a mass of merchant ships would make them more vulnerable, not less. It took over two months for Ll-G to wear down Jellicoe and he was less sure of himself than he implies in his *War Memoirs*. Nevertheless, by December 1917 the loss of merchant ships had been reduced to 170,000 tons that month compared to 300,000 tons the previous February. On Christmas Eve Admiral Jellicoe was sacked.

Prothero and Lee, encouraged by Ll-G, employed similar lateral thinking at the Board of Agriculture. When Lee read in a magazine that the American motor magnate Henry Ford was experimenting with a small tractor-plough for his own farm, Ll-G encouraged him to order 10,000 of them by cable. Ford built a factory in Detroit to carry out the order.

Much study is a weariness of the flesh, but conversations with a knowledgeable person stimulate and nourish one's mind.
LLOYD GEORGE

Over 250,000 women joined a new Women's Land Army that had an effect on morale similar to the Home Guard in the next World War. A new Ministry of Food was set up to organise a much fairer and reliable system of distribution. Lloyd George said that not only the army needed to march on its stomach but also those who stayed at home. He put in charge Lord Rhondda, a grocer's son from Merthyr Tydfil. Rhondda fixed prices for staple foods. Bread, for instance, was subsidised by the Treasury to the amount of £50 million a year so that a loaf cost 9d. This did not reduce queuing, a major grievance on the home front, so Rhondda decided to introduce rationing – a huge task. His prototype was the rationing scheme for sugar. By New Year's Day 1918 every household in the country was registered at its nearest grocer's shop, and the supply of sugar to each shop was calculated in relation to the number of persons registered, at a given rate per head. Soon meat, butter and margarine were rationed in the same way and a ration book was introduced in July. Given this meticulous organisation perhaps we should take for granted the statistic that whereas in February 1918 1,339,000 people were counted standing in London food queues, only one month later the figure had fallen to 15,000. It is another remarkable fact, though one repeated in the next war, that Britons were better fed during the war than before or after.

More was required than lateral thinking. The substantial increases in food production and the efficient distribution of food through rationing was a huge achievement of legislation and detailed organisation: the Ministry of Munitions writ even larger. The Corn Production Bill of August 1917 guaranteed minimum prices for wheat and potatoes subsidised by the government; established fixed minimum wages for agricultural workers; limited the rights of landowners to raise rents and empowered the Board to remove inefficient farmers from their tenancies. A new Ministry of Food was set up to organise a much fairer and reliable system of distribution.

'Whitehall is seething,' wrote Beatrice Webb in March 1917: 'The permanent officials, who in pre-war times lived demure and dignified lives, mildly excited here and there by departmental jealousies, are now fighting desperately for control. Each dept. has been handed over to the "interest" with which it is concerned. In that way our little Welsh attorney thinks you combine the least political opposition with the maximum technical knowledge. The Board of Trade is controlled by the ship owners, the Food Controller is a wholesale grocer, A Duke's land agent has been placed as the head of the Board of Agriculture.'[7]

Overshadowing 1917, indeed casting its shadow over the rest of the life of Lloyd George, lay the anguish of Third Ypres: Passchendaele, the 'battle of the mud'. 'Third Ypres was the blindest slaughter of a blind war,' concluded the historian

A J P Taylor. 'Haig bore the greatest responsibility. Some of the Flanders mud sticks also to Lloyd George, the man who lacked the supreme authority to forbid the battle.'[8] This is a grave charge, but true. In his *War Memoirs* Lloyd George takes over 100 pages trying to convince the reader, and himself perhaps, that he did all that was humanly possible to prevent the tragedy of Passchendaele. Over 300,000 British soldiers were killed or wounded between July and November 1917, yet again wasting their lives for a few miles of pulverised earth that were surrendered shortly afterwards. Did Lloyd George lack the courage of his convictions? Was it a failure in the system that the War Cabinet deferred to the Generals on matters of strategy? The answer was both.

The two senior generals in the British army were Haig and Robertson, the Commander-in-Chief and the Chief of the Imperial General Staff. Both were convinced 'Westerners' who believed that the war would be won or lost in battles of attrition on the Western Front. Neither liked Lloyd George, partly on the principle that civilians should mind their own business and partly on the personal grounds that he was not to be trusted. Robertson was a moral prig and Haig a social snob. 'Lloyd George seems to be astute and cunning', wrote Haig in his diary after their first meeting in 1916, 'with much energy and push, but I should think shifty and unreliable.'[9] His Chief of Staff, General Kiggell, used language that in the next war would be mocked as the prejudices of a red-faced Colonel Blimp: 'The Prime Minister poured out a lot of heretical, amateur strategy of the most dangerous and misleading kind … He is an under-bred swine.' Moreover, Robertson, whose job description was 'to be responsible for issuing the orders of the government in regard to military operations', in effect to be the interface at the highest level between the War Cabinet and General Headquarters (GHQ) in France, saw his loyalty

first to his Commander-in-Chief and only second to his Prime Minister. He witheld documents and schemed behind Ll-G's back. This was a grave weakness.

Lloyd George had weaknesses of his own. He felt ill at ease with officers, partly because he was a physical coward. He rarely visited the battlefields in France and later Flanders and when he had done so, in January 1916, it had seriously unnerved him. He had called in at a field hospital to see the son of an MP who was seriously wounded: 'The poor boy had been shot through the head, & the bullet had torn through part of his brain. He was in dreadful agony,' wrote Frances Stevenson. 'D's face was careworn and drawn when he arrived in London. *"I wish I had not seen him,"* he kept saying. *"I was not made to deal with things of war. I am too sensitive to pain and suffering, & this visit has almost broken me down".*'[10] Had Lloyd George steeled himself to visit the battlefields more, and shown the same confidence with the army officers that he did with everyone else, then the prejudice against him would have been much less.

The Prime Minister was determined not to authorise another slaughter like the Somme. His aim was to hold the line in Flanders and France until the French army had recovered from Verdun and until American troops arrived on the battlefields. (The United States declared war in April 1917.) Meanwhile there were softer targets on other fronts, conspicuously in 1917 the Italian/Austrian front near Trieste where Allied help could, thought Ll-G, knock Austria out of the war. But the War Policy Committee (WPC) allowed one exception to the strategy of maintaining a stalemate in the West and that was a campaign 'with a reasonable chance of success' defined according to the established criteria, of superiority in numbers, surprise, and limited objectives. When Haig and Robertson visited the WPC on 19 June they had such a campaign in mind; a campaign that had already begun with the capture of Messine Ridge to the south of the ruined city of Ypres and could proceed in stages to the capture of Zeebrugge, a major U-boat base. Lloyd George was suspicious from the start, and so were Bonar Law and Milner. They were not told that the French high command and several of Haig's own generals were highly sceptical, because Haig persuaded his subordinates to withhold this information. Even more culpable was Robertson who advised Haig to omit an appendix from his report about supposed weaknesses in the German Army because it was based on faulty intelligence.

In his *War Memoirs* Lloyd George was extremely rude about Haig. *He was intellectually and temperamentally unequal to the command of an Army of millions ... He had none of that personal magnetism that enables great leaders to inspire multitudes ... He was devoid of coherent expression ... He had no capacity for judging men.*[11] Whatever the truth of this, he omits the most important characteristic of Haig. He was a firm Calvinist who believed in Divine Providence, with himself as His agent. This made him self-confident and self-righteous. He believed that God was behind

Earl Haig of Bemersyde (1861–1928): Douglas Haig, born in Edinburgh, had a conventional officer's career, from Sandhurst to the 7th Hussars and then service in Egypt, South Africa, India and Northern France where he commanded the 1st Army Corps in 1914. In 1915 he became Commander of the British Expeditionary Force and from then on a controversial Field Marshal, although he always had the close support of George V. He waged a costly and exhausting war of attrition, for which he was much criticised by Lloyd George, but led the final successful offensive in 1918. After the war he organised the British Legion and devoted his time to the care of ex-servicemen.

his decisions. When things went wrong, as at Passchendaele, this had disastrous consequences.

The WPC held many meetings and Lloyd George continued to voice his doubts. Would not Third Ypres amount to *a brilliant preliminary success followed by weeks of desperate and sanguinary struggles with nothing to show except a ghastly casualty list?* But eventually Haig got his way. The crucial decision of Ll-G was that *he considered it too great a responsibility for the Committee to take the strategy of the war out of the hands of their military advisers. If after hearing his views they (the military advisers) still adhered to their previous opinion, then the responsibility for their advice must rest with them.*[12] Bonar Law and Milner agreed with this crucial acceptance of an advisory role and it needs to be added that most Conservative MPs also believed the army should be given a free hand. It was a responsibility Haig was happy to take. Although he was a democrat, he would try any tactic not to defer to the politicians and the politicians were not sufficiently resolute to override Haig and Robertson. Lloyd George admitted this in his *War Memoirs*: *The Government could have stopped it* [Third Ypres] *if they had the moral courage to do so. Had they done so, however, the Military Authorities would have insisted that they had been on the point of breakthrough, that the enemy was demoralised, and at the last moment they had been stopped by civilian politicians.*[13] The campaign of Third Ypres almost broke the British Army. When the village of Passchendaele, just a few kilometres north of Ypres, was eventually taken on 7 November only a ruin remained. Then Haig stopped the campaign: 'It has served its purpose.' Zeebrugge was a distant objective now too embarrassing to recall.

Lloyd George resolved that there would never be another Passchendaele. Both Haig and Robertson would have to go. He was unable to find a replacement for Haig, despite several attempts, but an opportunity of reducing his power presented itself in grave circumstances the following spring. On 21 March 1918 the Ludendorff offensive broke though the Allied lines and over the next two weeks the German army advanced an unprecedented 40 miles, capturing 1,200 square miles of ground. The attack almost split apart the British and French armies and the way to Paris seemed wide open. It was an unnerving time. On 24 March two friends of Lloyd George met the Prime Minister separately and recorded their accounts. Churchill entered in his diary: 'I never remember in the whole course of the war a more anxious evening. One of the qualities of Mr Lloyd George was his power of obliterating the past and concentrating his whole being on meeting the new situation. The resolution of the Prime Minister was unshaken under his truly awful responsibilities.' And George Riddell wrote: 'notwithstanding the news, the P.M. was firm and cheerful. Although very anxious and much worried he did not fail to have a good laugh. His courage is remarkable. His work and anxieties are always with him, but he mingles them with bright and amusing conversation which lightens the burden.'[14]

Adversity brought out the best in Lloyd George. He now acted decisively. On his own authority he dispatched all available British troops to France, increased the cross-Channel transports threefold and appealed to the US President Woodrow Wilson for help. As a result of Ll-G's appeal, General Pershing's American troops really entered the fighting for the first time, alongside the French, British and Dominion forces. According to A J P Taylor, 'Lloyd George's intervention was almost as decisive as had been his order for convoys the previous year'. Later, Ll-G sent out an inspirational message that was read out in theatres and cinemas: *To*

The 'Special Relationship' with the United States

The United States entered the War on 6 April 1917. From the start Lloyd George wanted a close relationship with President Wilson and that summer he wrote him a long and careful letter suggesting some kind of Allied joint council.

'Seeking a personal relationship, he said he did not wish his remarks *to have an official character.* He approached the role of the United States with care. *I fully appreciate the objections which the American people feel to being drawn into the complex of European politics. The British people have always attempted to keep themselves aloof from the endless racial and dynastic intrigues which have kept Europe so long in a state of constant ferment. These feelings must be far stronger in America. I have not, therefore, the slightest desire that the United States should surrender the freedom of action which she possesses at present ... [BUT] I believe that the presence at the deliberation of the Allies of independent minds, bringing fresh views, unbiased by previous methods and previous opinions, might be of immense value in freeing ourselves from the ruts of the past.*

If victory is to be obtained, it will only be because the great nations exhibit greater moral unity and greater tenacity in the last desperate days than the servants of an autocratic power. This depends more and more upon the British Commonwealth and the United States.

'Readers in the early twenty-first century will perceive in this letter the germ of what was to become a potent and pernicious theme in British foreign policy – the search for a 'special relationship' with the United States or the assumption that one already existed. Lloyd George suggests to the President that they should correspond as if they were personal friends, rather than merely as heads of government. In showing his appreciation of American reluctance *to be drawn into the complex of European politics*, he claims that it has always been Britain's traditional policy to stay *aloof* from Europe. He looks forward to a peace based upon close Anglo-American co-operation.'

[John Grigg, *Lloyd George, War Leader 1916–1918* (Penguin, London: 2003) pps 301–303.]

stop short of victory would be to compromise the future of mankind. I say 'Hold Fast'.

The Ludendorff offensive convinced Lloyd George that a unified Allied command was unavoidable. The following month Marshal Ferdinand Foch was appointed Commander-in-Chief of the Allied Armies in France. This put him in authority over Haig who, chastened for once by the German breakthrough, accepted it without question.

To stop short of victory would be to compromise the future of mankind. I say 'Hold Fast'.

LLOYD GEORGE

Under Foch's strategic direction the Allied armies finally stopped Ludendorff's offensive in July about 50 miles from Paris. The offensive had overreached itself and created a huge bulge (or salient), that the Allies attacked on three sides. The effect on German morale was disastrous: their decisive victory had not come, and the Allied reinforcements seemed endless while their troops were exhausted.

Although Lloyd George expected the war to last well into 1919, victory was only five months away. In fact the decisive day, what Ludendorff called 'the black day of the German Army', was 8 August when the British and Dominion counter-offensive near Amiens broke through and recaptured six miles of territory. This was the first of incessant short and sharp Allied attacks aimed for once at the German army's weak points rather than its strong ones. 'We have reached the limits of our capacity,' the Kaiser told Ludendorff. 'The war must be ended.'

Robertson had been fired in February 1918 and Haig had made no attempt to defend him. In fact he had no time for his subordinate, comparing him to 'a feather pillow, bearing the last marks of the person who sat on him'. There was a dramatic sequel. On 7 May a sensational letter appeared in four London papers written by Major-General Sir Frederick Maurice, the former Director of Military Operations at the War Office. In effect he accused Lloyd George of withholding troops from the Western Front with the result that the British Expeditionary Force had been left exposed to Ludendorff's offensive. Not surprisingly in the circumstances, Lloyd George reacted with fury and righteous indignation, although arguably there was some truth in the charge. He insisted on a major parliamentary debate and threatened to resign: *Make no mistake! This is a vote of censure.* He then used every trick in the book to explain complicated sets of figures to his maximum advantage. As a debater in full flow, torrents of words flooding out and eyes blazing, there was no one to match him. The vote of censure was heavily defeated although, to their cost, over 90 Liberal MPs voted against him. Maurice was disgraced but the man who had put him up to it was Sir William Robertson.

The previous summer Lloyd George had doubted that the German Army ever would be defeated in the west. Consistent with his belief that the Allies should attack on other fronts he insisted that a British army be assembled in Egypt for an attack on the Turks in Palestine and Mesopotamia (today's Iraq). He told its commander, General Edmund 'Bull' Allenby, to capture Jerusalem *as a Christmas present to the British nation.* This he did on 9 December 1917, after linking up with an irregular Arab army led by the Emir Feisal advised by the controversial British officer T E Lawrence. The entry into Jerusalem was carefully choreographed so as not to offend religious sensibilities. The conquerors entered on foot wearing ordinary khaki service dress; no flags were flown. But London did give itself a Christmas present. Bells were rung and *Te Deum*s sung in the cathedrals; Allenby was hailed as 'the Last Crusader'.

It was a propaganda victory for Lloyd George and this grew into a substantial victory when over the next five months Allenby's army drove the Turks out of the Middle East, culminating in the capture of Damascus in October. The Ottoman Empire surrendered. Lloyd George made the most of this British and Dominion victory (many of the troops were from Australia and New Zealand), expostulating to the French leader Georges Clemenceau later that month when he claimed a share: *Good heavens, the only assistance the French provided was a handful of niggers sent to see we did not steal the Holy Sepulchre.* He also argued with conviction that had the army in Egypt been reinforced in 1916 with *a few of the men we were wasting on the Somme* then the war might have been ended two *years before it finally dragged to its tragic close.* General Allenby, incidentally, remained a supporter of Lloyd George. When he was asked years later to join the protesters against Ll-G's treatment of Haig in his *War Memoirs* he refused: 'Attack Lloyd George? But I like the little man. He won the war, though for Heaven's sake don't tell him so.'

> 'Attack Lloyd George? But I like the little man. He won the war, though for Heaven's sake don't tell him so.'
>
> FIELD MARSHAL VISCOUNT ALLENBY
> OF MEGIDDO

As soon as the British army entered Palestine the War Cabinet needed to make a quick decision. It became a decision of fateful consequences. Should a 'national home' for the Jews of the Diaspora be provided in Palestine, as was urged on the government by the Zionist movement led in Britain by Dr Chaim Weizmann? If so what was to happen to the indigenous Arab population? In November 1917 the War Cabinet agreed the Balfour Declaration, though it could just as well have been the Lloyd George Declaration as Balfour was his Foreign Secretary: 'His Majesty's Government views with favour the establishment in Palestine of a national home for the Jewish people ... it being clearly understood that nothing shall be done which may prejudice the civil and religious rights of existing non-Jewish communities in Palestine.'

The rest is history. But what history forgets is that Lloyd George had in mind a Jewish state within the British Empire. As with the Boers or Welsh 20 years before he saw no contradiction between nationalism and imperialism; the Zionists would be an autonomous people yet subordinate to a larger loyalty. Asquith accused Lloyd George of 'not caring a damn for the Jews or their past or future', but that was not true. He had been brought up on the Bible and knew his Jewish history. The idea of returning the Jews to the land of their fathers appealed to him in a romantic way. Yet it was international Jewry that mattered also. America had just entered the war and Russia was in the throes of the Bolshevik revolution. Jews in both countries would be won over by Britain's support for Zionism. In February 1949 Dr Chaim Weizmann became the first President of Israel.

After the war, when Lloyd George was accused of betraying Liberal principles, he pointed to three measures he had passed despite the distractions of war that consolidated his reputation as a radical Liberal leader. The first was the Education Bill of 1918. This was the responsibility of the new President of the Board of Education, a former university Vice-Chancellor, H A L Fisher. He was another of Ll-G's inspired appointments, having the quality Ll-G admired of deciding what needed to be done and then getting on with it without fuss after Cabinet approval. They became lifelong friends. The Bill made compulsory the school leaving age of 14 and introduced the first national exam, the School Certificate that became the forerunner of the GCSE. Fisher was able to pour money into secondary education so that the number of teenagers staying on at school after 14 rose from 30,000 to 600,000.

The second reform was the Housing and Town Planning Bill of 1919 that started local authority housing, just in time to provide some *homes for heroes to live in*, Lloyd George's phrase that was to haunt him. Another of Ll-G's protégés, Dr Christopher Addison, who had made his mark at the Ministry of Munitions, steered this through.

The 1918 Representation of the People Act concluded the pre-war business of extending the franchise. All males over 21 and women over 30 were given the vote. This made Britain a truer democracy in one way but it missed an opportunity in another. Like most successful politicians, that is those that become ministers, Ll-G had little time for proportional representation (PR). It was *a device for defeating democracy* he said. Although a Speaker's conference during the war had

H A L Fisher (1865–1940): A distinguished historian, born in London, he was the biographer of Napoleon and Vice Chancellor of the University of Sheffield when Lloyd George summoned him to become President of the Board of Education in 1916. That year he became a 'coalition' Liberal MP and a lifelong supporter of the Prime Minister. He is best known for the Fisher Act of 1918 and his three-volume *History of Europe* in 1936. In between he was Warden of New College, Oxford, served on several commissions and was the first British delegate to the League of Nations in 1920.

unanimously recommended some form of PR and the House of Commons had showed support, Lloyd George had ignored it. Yet the lack of PR was to keep the Liberal Party out of government ever afterwards, despite winning between 20 and 30 per cent of the popular vote in many general elections.

On Monday 11 November at 10.55 a.m. a member of the Foreign Office gazed down from an upper window: 'Suddenly the front door of 10, Downing Street opened. Mr Lloyd George, his white hair fluttering in the wind, appeared upon the doorstep. He waved his arm outwards. He was shouting the same sentence over and over again. I caught his words. "At eleven o'clock this morning the war will be over." The crowd surged towards him. Plump and smiling he retreated behind the great front door. Now the crowd surged round the wall of the Downing Street garden. I observed Lloyd George emerge again, nervous and enthusiastic, and he stepped into the Parade. He waved his hands for a moment of gesticulation and the crowd patted feverishly at his back. Mr Lloyd George laughed heartily. It was a moving scene.'[15]

Chapter 4: The Man Who Made The Peace (1918–22)

With the national emergency nearing its end, Lloyd George needed to plan for a general election and decide whether to continue heading a coalition. He considered it unthinkable to return to the Liberals and serve under Asquith, and if he did so the Conservatives would win the election anyway and take credit for ending the war; equally unthinkable. As an advocate since 1910 of a non-party executive government he found it convincing to argue that the Coalition needed to continue because the national emergency would not end until the peace treaties were signed and reconstruction – *to make Britain a land fit for heroes to live in* – begun. Bonar Law had no objections to this: 'He can be Prime Minister for life if he likes,' he said. Nevertheless, Ll-G was convinced he was still a Liberal at heart and he did not wish to become a hostage to Conservative fortune so he determined to build up a power-base within the Liberal party – a dangerous move.

His advisers sounded out about 130 'Coalition Liberals' who would support him come what may and his Chief Whip, Freddie Guest, went about raising money to supply the necessary party machinery. His most controversial method was selling honours; knighthoods at £10,000 a time, baronetcies at £30,000 upwards and peerages from £50,000. This deeply offended those who took honours seriously, mostly those who already had their place in the medieval pecking order from the King downwards, but Ll-G could not care less. He was personally indifferent to this kind of reward and he argued that he simply made blatant the patronage that all prime ministers used to their advantage. He tried to make clear that the Fund, as he called it, was for party-political purposes and not his own.

More laudably, in 1917 Ll-G had introduced what Burke's Peerage called 'British Democracy's Own Order of Chivalry'. This was the Order of the British Empire (OBE) with five classes from GBE to BEM and although these classes were based on the social order, which makes them seem retrograde today, all the decorations were awarded for voluntary service. These were the 'people's honours' and for the first time the man and woman in the street qualified. The first recipient of the British Empire Medal, for example, was a munitions worker, Jenny Algar, whose citation read 'for presence of mind and good example on the occasion of an explosion at a shell filling factory'. The OBE was not for sale and within four years there were 25,000 recipients. Once again Ll-G had caught the popular mood.

Then Lloyd George made a deal with Bonar Law. All Coalition Liberals, defined mostly as those who had supported him in the Maurice debate, were promised a clear run at the forthcoming election; Conservative candidates would not oppose them. Asquith referred to this derisively as being given 'the coupon', as in food rations. 'My opinion,' wrote Hankey, 'is that the P.M. is assuming too much the role of a dictator and that he is heading for very serious trouble.'

The general election of 14 December 1918 has gone down in history as the 'coupon election'. During the campaign the euphoria of victory degenerated into the virulence of revenge. Stoked up by the *Daily Mail*, crowds yelled 'Make

Germany Pay', 'Hang the Kaiser' and 'Get Rid of Enemy Aliens'. At times Lloyd George gave into this, with serious consequences. His Final Manifesto before the election began simply: '1) Trial of the Kaiser. 2) Fullest indemnities from Germany'. Infected by the vehement mood he also lambasted the Labour Party as *an extreme pacifist Bolshevik group* (it had withdrawn its support as soon as the war was over); this too had lasting consequences. For the first time an alternative Labour Party contested a general election. This was the extreme right-wing, working man's National Democratic Party (NDP). Lloyd George over generously called its members *loyal working men* and gave them the 'coupon'. The NDP won 15 seats and although it quickly disappeared, it was the precedent for later war-mongering, racist parties in Britain that would be labelled fascist.

The overall result of the election, when three times as many people were eligible to vote as in 1911, was a colossal victory for Lloyd George and the Coalition, who won 478 out of 707 seats. Any effective opposition was left to Labour with 63 MPs. Only 28 'Asquithian Liberals' were elected and Asquith himself lost his seat. Hankey recorded that Ll-G 'is almost stunned by his overwhelming victory and seems really upset by Asquith's defeat'. It seemed that Lloyd George could do what he wanted but the truth was that, despite his Coalition Liberals, he was a prisoner of the Conservative Party. He said: *I have been told by some of my friends 'you are in favour of progressive legislation but you are surrounded by a reactionary bodyguard.' If reactionaries make it impossible to carry out a progressive policy I shall come back to the people and ask them to decide.* Alas, four years later the verdict was not what he expected.

The pressing business was to finish the war by turning the Armistice (literally 'short truce') into a peace treaty. All the victors agreed that Germany was responsible for starting the war and should pay for it. They also accepted two principles of Woodrow Wilson, the idealistic President of the United States. The first of these was that an international institution should be set up to maintain the peace, to ensure that the conflict just over really was 'the war to end all wars'. The second was that the defeat of the German, Austro-Hungarian and Ottoman Empires allowed for the boundaries of Europe to be redrawn in a more enlightened way; that oppressed nations with an ethnic and geographical identity should be given independence. 'Self-determination', it was called.

Woodrow Wilson (1856 – 1924): The 28th President of the United States (1913–21), he was born in Virginia of Scots-Irish parents and became first a lawyer and then a university professor at Princeton. Elected President by the Democrats in 1912 and again in 1916 he is chiefly remembered for his idealistic, pacifist 'Fourteen Points' which he brought to the Paris Peace Conference in 1919. His legacy was the League of Nations and his reward a Nobel Peace Prize that year. But the US Senate rejected the Treaty of Versailles and he died after a physical breakdown shortly afterwards.

So Lloyd George led an 'Empire delegation' of 400 to Paris where the new world order was to be decided. It commandeered the Hotel Majestic and insisted on its own staff and food. Ll-G himself stayed in a luxurious flat nearby with Frances Stevenson and his 16-year-old daughter Megan; who was chaperoning who was not clear. He took his own advisers and insisted that the Foreign Secretary Lord Curzon should stay behind in London. *Diplomats,* he opined, *were invented simply to waste time.* His own knowledge of the world was distinctly limited. *Who are the Slovaks? I can't seem to place them*, he queried. But as ever he seemed to relish the challenge: 'Whatever was going on at the conference, however hard at work and harried by the gravest responsibilities, Mr Lloyd George was certain to be at the top of his form – full of chaff intermingled with shrewd though never ill-natured comments on those with whom he was working', said a reluctant admirer, the Conservative adviser Lord Robert Cecil.

For the first six months of 1919 Paris was the centre of the world. Kings and queens, potentates and prime ministers of states past, present and putative attended the Quai D'Orsay. They awaited an audience with the Supreme Council of Four, the principal victors: 'It heard a procession of petitioners. Clemenceau slouched in his chair, frequently looking at the ceiling with a bored expression; Wilson fidgeted, getting up from time to time to stretch his legs; Lloyd George chatted in a loud undertone, making jokes and comments. The official interpreter, interpreted from French to English and back again, throwing himself into each speech as if he was begging for territory. The assistants tiptoed about with maps and documents. Every afternoon the doors opened and footmen carried in tea and macaroons.'[1] (The fourth member was Prime Minister Vittorio Orlando of Italy who rarely spoke unless Italian matters came up and eventually resigned in a huff.)

Diplomats were invented simply to waste time.

LLOYD GEORGE

After hearing the auditions, many of them mystifying – should the province of Teschen be allocated to the new state of Czechoslovakia or the revived state of Poland? Should Romania be given the Banat? – the Supreme Council referred the matter down to one of many commissions or sub-commissions for a recommendation, and then received it back for a decision. Regularly, plenary sessions were held of representatives from over 30 countries to consider a variety of international issues from a future League of Nations to the control of

waterways. These recommendations were also referred up to the Council. Only the defeated were not invited.

Woodrow Wilson irritated the others. He claimed that he represented the only country that had not entered the war for selfish reasons and therefore he saw himself as standing above the negotiations as arbitrator, some said pontificator. 'Talking to Wilson is something like talking to Jesus Christ', Clemenceau moaned. But as the weeks past the British and American delegates saw eye-to-eye, both complaining about the obsessive self-interest of the French. Lloyd George wrote in his *War Memoirs* that he found Clemenceau *a disagreeable and bad tempered old savage. He has no benevolence, reverence or kindliness*.

Nevertheless, both concurred with Wilson's first task for the Peace Conference, the setting up of a forum for world peace. So the League of Nations came into being though it never appealed to Lloyd George. He doubted that it would be effective and for this he had himself to blame.

Georges Clemenceau (1841–1929): French statesman and prime minister (1906–9, 1917–20), he was an intellectual iconoclast who trained as a doctor, worked as a teacher in the USA and became a brilliant journalist, founder of *L'Aurore*. He began his political career on the extreme left but ended as a fierce nationalist, nicknamed 'the Tiger'. He presided over the Paris Peace Conference in 1919 where his main contribution was an intransigent hatred of Germany.

The 'great powers', fearing that they might be outvoted by the smaller nations, insisted that nearly all decisions should be unanimous; and they did not allow the League to enforce arbitration or disarmament. But the key concern of the Supreme Council was Germany.

Here Lloyd George was in a fix. He had done his fair share of Hun-bashing, even suggesting that Kaiser Wilhelm II should be tried publicly at Dover Castle and shipped off to the Falkland Islands. He had promised before the 1918 election to *squeeze Germany until the pips squeaked*. Some of the MPs who elected him were 'hard faced men who look as if they have done very well out of the war' (so said a Conservative MP) and in April 1919 they demanded action. Over 200 Conservative MPs sent a telegram to Lloyd George in Paris reminding him of his words and telling him 'to present the bill in full'. They were supported vociferously and predictably by the *Daily Mail*; 'THE JUNKERS [Prussian war lords] WILL CHEAT YOU YET.' Nonetheless, Ll-G believed at heart that a savage retribution was morally wrong. He returned to Parliament and appealed to the MPs *not to soil this triumph of right by indulging in the angry passions of the moment, but to consecrate the sacrifice of millions to the permanent redemption of the human race from the agony of war*. Moreover he was statesman enough to realise that if *she* [Germany] *feels she has been unjustly treated in the peace of 1919 she will find means of exacting retribution from her conquerors*. Lloyd George set out his own views in the Fontainebleau memorandum, written with his closest advisers in March 1919. He argued that severe recriminations against Germany would create mass grievance at a time when Europe was destabilised by revolution and destruction. The French ignored this realistic overview.

Clemenceau's views were simple. The war had taken place in France and destroyed swathes of his country. France had paid up when Napoleon had been defeated and now France was going to collect, in full. Wilson agreed that Germany had started the war and should be punished, but when it came to deciding what the penalties should be he was unhelpful. Lloyd George saw himself as a moderating influence but he continued to vacillate. The result was a punitive settlement that Lloyd George regretted for the rest of his life. Indeed, he may be called the first 'appeaser' of Germany because after Versailles he spent many conferences trying to moderate its most severe clauses. The Germans called Versailles the 'treaty of shame' and they accepted it under protest. Germany alone was forced to admit 'war guilt' and Germany alone was required to disarm. Germany lost 13 per cent of its pre-war territory: Alsace-Lorraine and the Saar in the West, parts of Prussia and Silesia in the East. The French army occupied the Rhineland as a new border. Eventually, in 1921, the German war indemnity was agreed at 132 billion gold marks, that is, $34 billion. It paid back about 15 per cent of this before Hitler was appointed Chancellor and began systematically to reverse the Treaty.

Yet it is wrong to blame the Treaty of Versailles for causing the Second World War. For one thing, as the historian Margaret Macmillan wrote in *Peacemakers*, that ignores the decisions that everyone, politicians, diplomats, soldiers, even voters, made or did not make over the ensuing 20 years. Although it is the few clauses concerning the punishment, payment and prevention of Germany that are considered the most significant out of the 440 clauses of the Treaty of Versailles, it is the clauses in a subsequent treaty signed at San Remo the following that are most relevant today. It was convened to make peace in the Middle East. Here the Prime Minister was in expansive mood when chanced upon by his adviser Arnold Toynbee: 'Lloyd George, to my delight, had forgotten my presence and was thinking aloud. *"Mesopotamia ... yes ... oil ... irrigation ... we must have Mesopotamia; Palestine ... the Holy Land ... Zionism ... yes, we must have Palestine; Syria ... h'm ... what is there in Syria? ... Let the French have that".*'[2] The lands of the Bible, of the Greek myths, of the pathway to the British Raj, appealed to his romantic nature. Moreover, he was told that Mesopotamia contained the biggest oil fields in the world, a future asset that was fortunately lost on Clemenceau. 'When I want some oil,' he said, 'I'll find it at my grocer's.' Lloyd George did not want the French to lay claim to any territory the British Empire had liberated from the Turks.

The trouble was he had no clear idea what to do. In the end, he and Clemenceau awarded themselves 'mandates', a League of Nations term empowering Britain and France to govern countries not yet ready for independence. Britain got the mandates for Mesopotamia and Palestine, France for Syria. The trouble was that neither Palestine nor Mesopotamia was a nation, for they both lacked the ethnic and geographic identities necessary for self-determination. Mesopotamia, which Britain renamed Iraq, was an artificial construct of the three provinces of Baghdad, Basra and Mosul. It seethed with religious and racial disputes. The population was half Shia and a quarter Sunni Muslim, with Jews and Christians too; then there was the divide between Kurds, Arabs and Persians. Although Britain's mandate over Iraq ended in 1932 her influence continued. Britain is now paying the penalty for ignoring the true concept of self-determination it signed up to in 1919. In Palestine the British had to administer the increasing enmity between Jews and Arabs, complicated by the Balfour Declaration and the new state of Transjordan that denied Jews the right to build settlements on the east bank of that river. This, again, is a bitterly unresolved issue today that threatens world peace.

However, Lloyd George and the others did try and make the world a better place. They were required to answer huge questions that statesmen through the ages have been unable to answer. How do states control the passions of nationalism and religion? Can war be outlawed? They did not shirk these questions and their answers were more right than wrong. They could not predict the future.

Europe and the Treaty Of Versailles

'Lloyd George wanted to see Germany punished. At his moral core – and he had one in spite of what his enemies said – he deplored war and Germany had unleashed the worst one the world had ever seen. He was also, however, a statesman. *"If Germany feels she has been unjustly treated"*, he warned, *"she will find means of exacting retribution.* They must not drive Germany into a corner. *The greatest danger that I see is that Germany may throw in her lot with Bolshevism and place her brains, her resources, her vast organising power at the disposal of revolutionary fanatics whose dream is to conquer the world.* He urged the peacemakers to make a moderate peace that would last.

The French were furious ... Illusion or not, the British were determined to disengage themselves from the continent and its problems. A balance of power there had always served Britain well; intervention was only needed when a single nation threatened to dominate the whole. Germany had been that threat but it would be foolish now to destroy it and leave France supreme. As passions cooled, the British remembered both their old rivalry with France and the potential for friendship between Britain and Germany. British industry needed markets; there were 70 million Germans. Britain wanted stability on the continent, not the sort of chaos that could be so clearly seen further east; a solid Germany at Europe's centre could provide that. Lloyd George's much-criticized change of heart on the peace terms reflected a general British ambivalence.

Clemenceau now appeared to be hardening his position on Germany. Britain and the United States, he pointed out, were protected by the sea. "We must have an equivalent on land". He demanded the Saar and the military occupation of the Rhineland. "The Germans are a servile people who need force to support an argument". With some reluctance Lloyd George agreed with the Rhineland clauses ... although he was well aware that, in the long run, it was not in Britain's best interests to have a weak and possibly revolutionary Germany at the heart of Europe.'

[Margaret MacMillan, *Peacemakers* (John Murray, London: 2002) pp 199, 208–9]

'Ll-G used to say that the happiest time of his life was the six months he spent in Paris during the conference,' wrote Frances Stevenson. 'The worry of the war was finished; the framing of the peace brought out all his art and skill as a negotiator.' Now this skill was needed in other avenues. A view of these post-war years is of Lloyd George endlessly involved in crisis negotiations – threatened strikes today, war in Ireland tomorrow – instead of implementing his vision of a land fit for heroes to live in. In part he was a victim of the forces that were bound to follow an all-consuming war and in part of people's expectations that he had encouraged. Moreover, he followed his own inclinations, for crisis management was what he did best, out in front on his own, instead of relying on a solid team, a political party, behind him.

Ll-G's first appearance before the new House of Commons in 1919 was unsettling: *I felt, as I looked in front of me, that I was addressing a Trades Union Congress. Then when I turned round, I felt I was speaking to a Chamber of Commerce.* The stereotype confrontation of cloth cap versus bowler hat was emerging. The gap between the 'haves' and the 'have nots' had been as great before the war but now the 'have nots' were more powerful than ever before. In 1920, of the 15 million manual workers in the country, over eight million were members of trade unions. That year the General Council of the Trades Union Congress joined with the National Executive of the Labour Party and the Parliamentary Labour Party to form a National Council of Labour. It spoke for 'Labour' throughout the country. It was a new and formidable body.

Neither Labour nor Conservative parties wanted to keep wartime controls. Let wealth and freedom grow together! Price controls were ended (rationing remained until 1921), restrictions were removed from foreign trade and direction from industry. Consequently prices rose twice as fast in 1919 as in the war years and although wages soared after them, strikes proliferated also. With Ll-G in Paris the government dealt as best it could with striking gas and electricity workers, railwaymen, police, dockers and miners. A new militancy was in the air after the obedience of the war years.

Many thought a Bolshevik revolution was imminent. The British Communist Party held its founding meeting in July 1920 and called for a revolution. For some time the new Minister of War, Winston Churchill, had been urging Lloyd George to declare war on Bolshevik Russia as the home of revolution. The tension increased in July 1920 when the Red Army advanced on Warsaw with the slogan 'To the West! Over the corpse of White Poland lies the road to world-wide conflagration'. The next month the new dockers' leader Ernest Bevin, speaking for the TUC, threatened a general strike if war was declared on Russia, with the slogan 'Hands Off Soviet Russia!' Lloyd George was only too happy to back down, knowing that the war-weariness of the British would not stand for another conflict. Anyway, the Poles drove the Red Army back. Lloyd George moved Churchill sideways to the Colonial Office.

The miners were ready for some kind of class war too. The Sankey Commission recommended (narrowly) that the mines should remain nationalised, as in the war years, but in 1919 Lloyd George rejected the proposal. A year later, feeling betrayed, the Miners' Federation demanded more pay and threatened to strike with the dockers and railway men in a Triple Alliance that could paralyse industry. A tired and irritable Lloyd George wrote to Bonar Law on 4 September: *We must show Labour that the Government mean to be masters.* In October an Emergency Powers Bill was rushed through parliament setting up a permanent anti-strike apparatus, civil and military. Lloyd George, whose negotiating style was often to talk tough but then do a deal, agreed with the miners' demand. But this was only a truce. In March 1921 the mines were returned to the unfettered capitalism of private ownership, making further confrontation inevitable. Lord Birkenhead, the Lord Chancellor, said 'I should call them [the Miners' Federation] the stupidest men in England if I had not previously had to do with the owners.' The miners asked for more money again. The owners refused. The miners went on strike. This time the Prime Minister, by adroit brinksmanship, kept the Triple Alliance apart so that the other two unions pulled out on 15 April 1921; 'Black Friday' in Labour history. 'The PM in great form as the day went in his favour,' a civil servant reported to Bonar Law. The strike collapsed.

We must show Labour that the Government means to be masters.

. LLOYD GEORGE TO BONAR LAW

The post-war boom ended suddenly in the winter of 1920. Manufacturers had expected a huge demand for the products they had not been able to sell during the war, but from the Pyrenees to the Urals Europeans were living in chaos and poverty. The European export market scarcely existed. At the same time Lloyd George accepted that the government could not sustain the vast overspend of the war when a debt of £2,000 million had been incurred. He reduced government spending from £2,700 million in 1917–18 to just over £1,000 million in 1920–1, a drastic slash of over 60 per cent. Then he increased taxation to an all-time high of £1,400 million. The next year, in February 1922, Sir Eric Geddes completed the cuts by wielding his 'axe', as it was called, at several of the government departments that had remained bloated since the war years. Much to Ll-G's dismay he also slashed Fisher's and Addison's education and housing plans. In fact Addison had already resigned (in June 1921), goaded by the press barons, particularly Northcliffe, who financed

'Anti-Waste' candidates to stand at by-elections. Unemployment rose sharply from 350,000 in April 1920 to 2.5 million in July 1921, after which it settled at 1.4 million for the rest of the 1920s. One result was that industrial disputes declined. The number of working days lost through strikes in 1921 amounted to a colossal 86 million but this went down to 20 million the following year, and continued to fall.

Behind the arid figures, of course, lay human suffering. In November 1921 a vast demonstration of 25,000 ex-soldiers marched on the Cenotaph to place a wreath inscribed: 'From the living victims – the unemployed – to our dead comrades who died in vain.' The banners were covered with the medals of those who wore pawn tickets instead on their lapels. Britain was no land fit for heroes. Ll-G felt badly about ex-servicemen in particular. Despite the economic climate he increased the coverage of his 1911 insurance scheme to include the short-term unemployed in most industries and he widened the scope to include allowances for wives and families. He made sure Parliament voted £1 million to assist the passages of ex-servicemen who wished to emigrate to the Dominions. Nevertheless, he was blamed for the misery of the depression. To many he was no longer the 'People's David' but the friend of capitalist bosses like the mine owners and the ally of Red-baiting politicians like Churchill. His dismissal of the Labour Party as *an extreme pacifist Bolshevik group* was not forgiven.

There was some truth in the allegation that Lloyd George had moved away from the people. His mindset was moving to the right at this time. He had always admired captains of industry, enjoyed the company of the *nouveaux riches* like himself, but now as his friend Riddell observed: 'He is steadily veering over towards the Tory point of view. He constantly refers to the great services rendered by captains of industry and defends the large share of profits they take. He says one

Leverhulme or Ellerman is worth more to the world than, say, 10,000 sea captains or 20,000 engine drivers ... His point of view has entirely changed.'[3]

Throughout 1921 and 1922, Lloyd George supposedly spent half his time on foreign affairs, a fifth on domestic matters and the remaining third on Ireland. Ireland was the graveyard of the Liberal Party. From Gladstone onwards the Party had divided and wearied itself in the cause of Home Rule, to no avail. At heart it was unable to cope with Ulster, Protestant and Loyalist, dedicated to the historic call of 'no surrender'. Soon after he became Prime Minister, Lloyd George told Parliament that he, at least, realised the intractability of the problem: *Ireland is no more reconciled to British rule than she was in the days of Cromwell ... It has to do with the pride and self-respect of the people. I entreat the House of Commons to get that well into its mind ... The other fact is that in the north east portion of Ireland you have a population as hostile to Irish rule as the rest of Ireland is to British rule ... as alien in blood, in religious faith, in traditions, in outlook, as alien from the rest of Ireland as the inhabitants of Fife or Aberdeen.*[4]

Before he had become Prime Minister he had lost a rare opportunity of a settlement. At Easter 1916 a small group of Irish rebels had seized the Dublin General Post Office and proclaimed an Irish Republic. The rebellion had been put down with great severity, leaving everyone in a state of shock. Asquith had asked Ll-G to 'see his way to Ireland' where a 'unique opportunity' for settlement presented itself. And so it had proved. Lloyd George had persuaded the leader of the Irish National Party, John Redmond, to accept Home Rule for the 26 counties of the South and West of Ireland while

Ireland is no more reconciled to British rule than she was in the days of Cromwell.

LLOYD GEORGE

six counties in the North and East would remain, for the time being at least, part of Britain. In fact both sides had accepted the deal, but Asquith with typical indecision had failed to formulate this speedily into a bill for Parliament. Lloyd George had done nothing, opposition had grown and the chance had been lost.

Now, in 1919, Redmond was discredited and dead. Sinn Fein ('ourselves alone') had replaced the Irish National Party because Sinn Fein would make no concessions. After the general election of 1918 those of its MPs who were not in gaol established their independent parliament, the Dail, in the Dublin Mansion House and pretended that British rule from the Castle did not exist. Under their President, Eamonn De Valera, the one surviving ringleader from 1916, the Dail solemnly renewed the proclamation of a Republic made two years before from the Post Office. But Sinn Fein was no small group of rebels. It was backed by the Irish Republican Army (IRA) of several thousand active fighters, financed from the United States and armed from Europe.

When Lloyd George proscribed Sinn Fein and dismantled the Dail an irregular war broke out between the Royal Irish Constabulary and the IRA. It was a war of terror, of executions and reprisals, ambushes and burnings. Ll-G announced *you do not declare war against rebels* and called for a civilian army of ex-servicemen *to take murder by the throat.* So a volunteer force of 'Black and Tans' countered violence with violence. Martial law was declared but the violence intensified and spread to England. Asquith said: 'Things are being done in Ireland which would disgrace the blackest annals of the lowest despotism in Europe.' Lloyd George attempted one of his adroit and creative solutions by steering through Parliament a Government of Ireland Act that set up separate parliaments in Belfast and Dublin, and a Council of Ireland composed of representatives from both. It decreed that the 'Imperial Parliament' at Westminster would control the police, defence and foreign policy. This drastic measure made no difference. The 'troubles' continued and Lloyd George was at the end of his tether.

Then, completely unexpectedly, a solution presented itself. On 22 June 1921, despite the risk of assassination, King George V travelled to Ulster and opened Stormont with a conciliatory speech that called on his Irish subjects to 'forgive and forget'. This royal magnanimity was well received. Lloyd George invited de Valera to London and to his relief and surprise de Valera agreed at once. It turned out that, unknown to outsiders, the IRA was down and almost out. Its commander Michael Collins said afterwards: 'you had us dead beat. We could not have lasted another three weeks.' So negotiations began. They were not so much about Ulster because by now most Irish nationalists recognised that Ulster would be lost to the Irish Free State and most Ulster Unionists realised that the union would end. They were more about the form of Irish 'allegiance' to the Crown and Empire. De Valera wanted a 'free association'; Lloyd George was determined to defend 'the Empire'. Over the next six months Lloyd

The Black and Tans: During the Irish War of Independence, 1919–21, the Irish Republican Army targeted the Royal Irish Constabulary (RIC). Rather than admit a war on British territory the government augmented the RIC with volunteer ex-servicemen instead of regular troops. They wore khaki uniforms, with the black belts and dark green caps of the RIC, hence their nickname. Their aim was to 'make Ireland a hell for Rebels to live in'. This they did, burning and murdering to the tune of 'We are the boys of the RIC, as happy, happy, as can be'. International concern at the dirty war with the IRA led to the Anglo-Irish Treaty.

George used every negotiating skill in his vast repertoire. He humoured de Valera by pointing out to his fellow Celt that neither in Irish nor Welsh was there a word for 'republic'.

He bullied the British Cabinet by summoning it to Inverness when he was on holiday. He tricked the Irish delegation by hinting privately that Ulster would eventually join the Irish Free State, as it was due to be called, because the commission summoned to decide the Irish border would so whittle down Ulster as to make it unworkable. On 5 December he threatened the Irish with renewing war unless there was agreement in three days. During the evening of 6 December he practised the ultimate brinkmanship by brandishing in front of the delegation, still wavering, two letters to James Craig, the Unionist leader. One declared war, the other peace; *which letter am I to send? We must know your answer by ten tonight.* The Irish signed the Articles of Agreement at 2.00 a.m. on 7 December. According to Ll-G, Michael Collins *looked like a man who was signing his own death warrant.*

Michael Collins (1890–1922): Born in County Cork he was interned in England after the Easter Uprising and became a Sinn Fein MP in 1918. In the War of Independence he was also intelligence chief of the IRA. Determined to make peace, he negotiated the Anglo-Irish Agreement of 1921 that established the Irish Free State. This, however, split Sinn Fein and led to civil war. Collins, Commander of the Free State Army, was killed in an ambush by Republicans opposed to the treaty. 300,000 people lined the streets of Dublin as his funeral cortege passed.

And so it proved. Sinn Fein was divided whether or not to accept the Treaty. President de Valera, who was opposed, resigned and Collins was killed in the ensuing civil war. Nevertheless, the Irish Free State came into existence precisely one year after the signing of the Treaty. It did not include

Ulster and all members of the Dail were required to swear an oath 'acknowledging the common citizenship of Ireland with Great Britain'. The King appointed a Governor-General. Nevertheless, the Irish Free State now had its own government and more independence than the pioneers had dreamed of. It also had Dominion status, like Canada.

For Lloyd George it was a triumph. He could claim to have solved the Irish Question that had bedevilled his predecessors since Pitt the Younger at the end of the 18th century. It would remain in the background of British politics until the renewal of the 'Troubles' in the 1960s. In the end, wholesale it was the weariness with bloodshed that brought peace. As the Irish negotiator Arthur Griffith said, defending the Treaty: 'I was told, "No, this generation might go down, but the next generation might do something or other". Is there to be no living Irish nation?' He died a few months later. Lloyd George did not enjoy his triumph either. Liberal and Labour voters did not forgive him for the Black and Tans and Conservative unionists considered he had surrendered to IRA violence.

By 1922 Lloyd George had many enemies, though considering the enormity of the problems he had to solve this was inevitable. He made things worse, however, by his autocratic and arbitrary methods. He practised crisis government and in between, complained his new secretary, A J Sylvester, it was 'the same old muddle and mess'. In March 1922 Ll-G sacked Lord Montague, Secretary of State for India, who got his revenge with a telling speech delivered to the Cambridge Liberal Club:

I must have peace and quiet. I cannot get away from people. There is a fresh crisis every day.

LLOYD GEORGE

'The head of our government is a Prime Minister of great but eccentric genius. He has demanded the price which it is within the power of every genius to demand – the complete disappearance of the doctrine of Cabinet responsibility. He is a great genius – but a dictator.'[5] The Prime Minister was tired and talked of resignation. He said to Riddell: *I must have peace and quiet. I cannot get away from people. There is a fresh crisis every day.*

His position was insecure. The War Cabinet had been dissolved in October 1920 and Bonar Law, his loyal and effective deputy, had resigned through ill-health in March 1921. His attempts to start a new centre party were floundering. Apart from Bonar Law, few were interested in 'fusion'. The Coalition Liberals still regarded themselves at heart as Liberals and would not 'fuse' with the Conservatives. The Asquithian Liberals were resolutely anti-Lloyd George, so they remained a small and independent body without a leader, hence known as the 'Wee Frees'. The Conservatives increasingly saw Lloyd George as a liability. The Ulster Unionists cordially mistrusted him and wanted a return to normality.

Lloyd George had grown away from party politics and rarely attended Parliament. On his many trips to conferences abroad (over 20 in the three years after Paris) he took with him his own experts, primarily Maurice Hankey, the former War Cabinet Secretary, and Phillip Kerr, a founder-member of the 'Garden Suburb', while as usual leaving his Foreign Secretary Lord Curzon behind. Curzon wrote to his wife in April 1921: 'He wants his Forn. Sec. [*sic*] to be a valet, almost a drudge, and he has no regard for the civilities of official life.' The insecurity of Lloyd George's position in part accounted for his autocratic style. He had few friends in the Cabinet and he had no political party behind him: so he ran the country in his own way.

The three 'Press Lords', Northcliffe (*The Times* and *Daily*

Mail), his brother Rothermere (*Daily Mirror*) and Beaverbrook (*Daily Express*) were mostly against him. Their papers made the most of an 'Honours scandal' in the summer of 1922 when they reported with glee that a shadowy figure called Maundy Gregory had been caught selling honours in London nightclubs. One recipient of a peerage was a South African businessman, Sir Joseph Robinson, who had been fined £500,000 for fraudulent practices. The press hinted that the Prime Minister was pocketing the money himself. It did not seem scandalous to any of the Press Lords that they had all been made viscounts or barons under the same system. The honours scandal reinforced a widely held view that Ll-G's government was slipshod and sleazy. 'Taffy was a Welshman, Taffy was a thief', Beatrice Webb wrote in her diary caustically.

Lord Curzon (1859–1925): George Nathaniel Curzon had an aristocratic upbringing in Kedleston Hall, Derbyshire as son of Baron Scarsdale. His style was suited to imperial roles and his time as Viceroy of India (1888–1905) saw him at his grandest. He persuaded the government to invade Tibet and relished the pomp of his position, although he was pro-Indian and a reformer. In 1916 Lloyd George appointed him to his War Cabinet and then as Foreign Secretary in 1919 where he remained until 1924, displaying a detailed knowledge of foreign affairs. He frequently clashed with Lloyd George, who disliked his egotism, and was crushed when he failed to succeed Bonar Law as prime minister in 1923.

It was, improbably, a small town on the Turkish coast that precipitated the downfall of Lloyd George. Since the collapse of the Ottoman Empire, Allied troops had occupied Constantinople and the Dardanelles. A resurgent Turkey led by Kemal Atatürk, based at Ankara in Anatolia, was trying to win back its territory. Ll-G hated the Turks and had encouraged the Greeks to occupy Smyrna, the main port on the West Turkish coast. In September 1922 Ataturk's army slaughtered the Greeks in Smyrna and advanced on Chanak where a small British garrison was holed-up guarding the Dardanelles. On 29 September Lloyd George and Churchill, who could not resist a good scrap, telegrammed the garrison that the British government was, in effect, about to declare war on Turkey. They had no Cabinet approval for this and very few wanted Britain to be brought to the brink of war. Once again it seemed that Ll-G was out of control, a Welsh wizard whose pyrotechnic displays were about to cause a conflagration. From retirement, Bonar Law wrote to *The Times* saying that Britain could not act alone as 'the policeman of the world'. The press was unanimously hostile. Luckily the garrison ignored the telegram and arranged a conference. The government was tottering, as Lloyd George recognised. He said in Manchester on 12 October; *If there is a change believe me no-one would welcome it more than I would.*

This new crisis came at a time when the Cabinet was planning to call a general election with Lloyd George standing once again as head of the Coalition. Austen Chamberlain, Bonar Law's successor as Leader of the Conservative Party, realised that Lloyd George was not popular and said privately that he would replace him after the election. However, at a mass meeting of his MPs at the Carlton Club on 19 October he gave the impression that he would be happy if Lloyd George stayed in power indefinitely. That caused uproar. The rising star, Stanley Baldwin, called Ll-G a 'dynamic force – a very terrible thing', meaning that although he 'got things done' he had a destructive effect on political life. Even Bonar Law, whose patience Lloyd George had tried too often, spoke in favour of ending the coalition. By 185 votes to 88 the Conservatives resolved to fight the election as an independent party. Chamberlain resigned. White-faced he hurried back to Downing Street where he found Ll-G and Frances Stevenson in the Cabinet room. 'We must resign, Ll-G,' he announced, 'Baldwin has carried the meeting.'

Lloyd George seemed pleased to go but then he did not realise he would never return. In fact he doubted that the Conservatives would win the general election as an independent party and he must have thought his departure was very temporary. On 23 October he submitted his resignation to George V who expressed genuine regret and also assumed he would be back at some stage if not immediately. After all, he had dominated British politics for years and he was not yet 60. That afternoon Ll-G said his farewells to Downing Street.

Austen Chamberlain (1863–1937): One of the Birmingham Chamberlain dynasty, son of the Leader of the Liberal Unionists and brother of a future Conservative prime minister, his aloofness and high principals made him a natural second in politics. He was the only Leader of the Conservative Party in the 20th century until William Hague not to become prime minister. In 1922 he opposed the removal of Lloyd George and resigned on principal, thus losing his chance of becoming prime minister in the general election that followed. He was Chancellor of the Exchequer 1903–5 and 1919–21; Foreign Secretary and Deputy Prime Minister 1925–9.

'He was full of fun' said a secretary, pretending he was now a minor politician leading a deputation to the new Prime Minister: *We have come to ask for a grant for Welsh education and on behalf of the refugees from Smyrna*, **he** pleaded in a voice of self-mockery. At 4.00 p.m. he motored away with his son Gwilym to Churt, smiling to the last.

Part Three

THE LEGACY

Chapter 5: The Leader in Waiting (1922–31)

The age of Baldwin and MacDonald began in 1922 and ended in 1937. They alternated as Prime Minister and then shared office. They were similar men of decency, indeed benevolence, and similarly incapable of offering the leadership and radical policies necessary to lift Britain out of the Depression. They liked each other and hated Lloyd George. When Macdonald became Prime Minister in 1924 he asked 'Honest Stan' Baldwin for his photograph to hang on the wall at Chequers, the Prime Minister's country house originally acquired for Lloyd George in 1918; as for Ll-G's photo, he put it away in a drawer because 'it makes me see red'. Baldwin confessed he was 'obsessed' with Lloyd George. Indeed, much of his policy was motivated to keep him out of office, whatever the result. The truth was that Lloyd George was not on the sidelines of politics but still, literally, at the centre. He was rightly suspected of conspiring towards various party alliances or coalitions of the centre ground and therefore he was at the centre of his opponent's calculations. Yet he was far more than a scheming politician. He towered over the age: the statesman who had been both a great social reformer and war leader. To many he was the man for an emergency, restlessly waiting and plotting his call. As Macdonald said, 'the Goat is kicking vigorously'.

He was, however, still a scapegoat for the broken promises of 1918 and 1919. Even ten years later the *Evening Standard* reported during the general election campaign of 1929: 'Real hostility seems to be roused wherever Lloyd George's name is mentioned. "Where are the Homes for Heroes?" "Who promised to hang the Kaiser?" "What about squeezing Germany till the pips squeak?" All the old war cries are now used to confound the Liberal candidates.' In fact Lloyd George was hated most among his fellow Liberals. Many had not forgiven him for deserting Asquith in 1916 and even more resented him, once he returned to the party in 1923, for refusing to transfer his notorious war chest to Liberal coffers. When Asquith died in 1928 Lloyd George paid a double-edged tribute in the House of Commons: *He died on the banks of the Thames. He was a kindred spirit – placid, calm, moving with a stately and serene flow, never turbulent even in the worst of weather*. This provoked Lady Margot Asquith to write a vicious letter to Baldwin: 'Ll-G counts for nothing. He counts in our party because we have no money. Thank God it was your party that made him rich. He is the greatest Bluff ever put upon a foolish public. Every time you say the Liberals have no leader *I bless you*. The pseudo-leader betrayed his master.'

In fact Lloyd George was paying the price of putting country before party in 1916. For seven years his only power-base was a dwindling band of Coalition then National Liberals, as they called themselves in 1922. Moreover, he was not adept at party politics despite his constant scheming. The very skill that served him so well in office, the ability to get things done by brokering

'He {Lloyd George} is no doubt genuinely patriotic and public-spirited, but all his ways are crooked and he is obsessed with a craving for power.'

BEATRICE WEBB

a deal, was counterproductive when he was out of office; it simply made him resented. Beatrice Webb wrote in her diary: 'He is a blatant intriguer, and every thing he says is of the nature of an offer "to do a deal". He neither likes nor dislikes you; you are a mere instrument, one among many, sometimes of value, sometimes not worth picking up. He is no doubt genuinely patriotic and public-spirited, but all his ways are crooked and he is obsessed with a craving for power.'[1]

With hindsight this period is a Lloyd George tragedy. Despising the prime ministers, desperate to 'get things done', he was reduced to scheming in the corridors of power. As the Depression worsened towards the end of the decade so he became convinced that he had evolved a policy, a vision that could lift Britain out of it. Yet mediocre politicians who acted out of insecurity and spite as much as anything else frustrated him. As ever the cry was that Lloyd George was not to be trusted. It has to be said that not only his scheming and spinning of words, but also his scandalous love life and his expensive lifestyle, contributed to this. The Goat was in the wilderness.

The image of Lloyd George that has stuck, the little man with the untidy white hair squashed under a bowler hat, sporting a bushy moustache and walking with a stick, comes from these years. 'Are you Charlie Chaplin?' a little girl asked. He was now less benevolent than he looked, more irascible and spiteful. But his extraordinary capacity to mesmerise an audience was still there. 'L-G sparkled, revolved and coruscated with his sensitive antennae feeling in all directions,' wrote Oswald Mosley in 1931. He spent much of the time living at Churt, the house he built in Surrey in 1922 and called *Bron-y-de*, 'Breast of the South'. Here he was looked after by Frances Stevenson ('Pussy'), by now his virtual second wife and in 1929 the mother of his second living daughter,

Jennifer. His first daughter, Mair, had died in 1907 and his remaining daughter by Margaret, Megan, who took after her father, was elected Liberal MP for Anglesey in 1929. She had discovered the true relationship of her father with her former governess in 1920 and ever after regarded Frances Stevenson with hatred. Although Lloyd George wrote affectionately to Margaret, his *hen gariad* ('old darling'), he seldom visited Wales and Frances was now his consoler and carer; but his promiscuity continued. At Churt he established a fruit farm and proudly walked politicians round the orchards, claiming that he had the hill farms of Wales in his blood and preaching that the husbandry of the land was essential for the survival of the nation.

When Lloyd George was voted out of 10 Downing Street in October 1922 he said *the burden is off my shoulders, but my sword is in my hands*. He kept his parliamentary seat as a National Liberal backbencher in the general election the next month which was won by Bonar Law for the Conservatives. He relished his absence from responsibility and spent the next year writing for the newspapers, from which he earned a massive £30,000, and travelling round the United States, where he was the most popular visitor since Charles Dickens. He returned to find that Baldwin (Bonar Law had resigned through ill-health) was holding a surprise general election on the traditional Tory issue of 'protectionism' (trade tariffs). Baldwin feared, quite wrongly, that 'the Goat' had been converted to protectionism by his American experience and was about to return advocating the same thing as the remedy for the depressed economy, so he got in first. His motive, typical of his obsession with Ll-G, was to 'dish the Goat'. This seemed the moment for Lloyd George to re-unite with Asquith's Liberals to champion their traditional cause of free trade. He agreed to serve as Asquith's deputy but there was no love lost between them, particularly when he refused to hand over that constant bone of contention, his Fund. As in the next election a year later he thought that the Liberals had no hope of power and no new policies. He preferred to bide his time and keep his war chest locked.

Although the Conservatives won the election of 1923, they had no clear majority and it was a simple matter for the Liberals to unite with the Labour Party and turn them out of office in January 1924. This brought in the first Labour government in British history but there was no chance of collaboration between MacDonald and Lloyd George. Their mutual dislike put paid to that. *Ramsay uses words as though they were sounds, not weapons*, said Ll-G in a telling phrase. More significant was his dislike of socialism and his determination to reshape the Liberal party in his own image. Without Liberal support Labour could not govern either. In November 1924 MacDonald lost office on a vote of confidence and Baldwin was returned to power, this time with a huge majority: the Liberals won only 40 seats.

Ramsay [MacDonald] *uses words as though they were sounds, not weapons.*

LLOYD GEORGE

Lloyd George became leader of the Liberal Party two years later. The General Strike of 1926 was the most momentous event of the decade and one of its lesser ramifications was to serve as a catalyst in the mistrustful, hateful arena of Liberal politics. Asquith deplored the Strike, thinking it might lead to revolution. Lloyd George's sympathies were with the strikers and he counselled negotiation. When he stayed away from a meeting of the Shadow Cabinet, Asquith sacked him. This was an extraordinary over-reaction that may only be explained by the rumour that Ll-G was thinking of transferring his Fund to Labour. There was no truth in this but, as ever, the Goat could not resist butting or nuzzling other animals in the farmyard. He had been scheming for some kind of tie with Labour but nothing more. *A Liberal I was born, and a Liberal I shall die*, he protested. The Liberal membership and the majority of MPs believed him, although the Shadow Cabinet did not. Asquith had lost control of his part of the farmyard and had no option but to resign himself. He did so, deploring 'our weaklings who are going a-whoring after Ll-G'. Thus ended the longest political duel since Gladstone and Disraeli. But for some time Asquith had only the past to offer while Lloyd George had a future.

'When Ll-G came back to the party, ideas came back to the party,' said a former Liberal opponent, C F G Masterman. Once again, Ll-G's creative energy, his determination to find solutions and his radical thinking combined to produce the most important party programme between the wars. It came in a variety of colours, lengthy policy documents called 'the Green book' (*The Land and the Nation*, 1925), 'the Yellow book' (*Britain's Industrial Future*, 1928) and 'the Orange book' (*We Can conquer Unemployment*, 1929). These amounted to the regeneration of the land through 'cultivating tenure' (always close to Ll-G's heart), whereby local authorities took over land and leased it to those wanting to farm it; the beginnings of industrial democracy through shareholder and worker power backed up by government planning; and a massive and thoroughly argued case for public investment on public works. Once again Lloyd George showed his talent for choosing outside experts, since this huge programme to lift Britain out of the Depression was formulated by committees who had gathered at Liberal summer schools since 1921. Ll-G's former critic John Maynard Keynes was foremost among them. Their philosophical quest was to find a way between the irresponsible freedom of capitalism and the lack of individual freedom in socialism. Roosevelt's New Deal in the United States and

Attlee's planning of a mixed economy after 1945 owed much to this pioneering programme.

Tragically, in the general election of 1929 the voters did not share this vision. Admittedly, the ideas that prosperity came from spending money and that unemployment could be ended by the government creating jobs were hard to understand. When the promises came from the same Welsh Wizard who had promised to build a land fit for heroes to live in, then surely the 'safety-first' of Baldwin or the 'no-monkeying' of MacDonald were better options? Despite optimistic forecasts the Liberals won only 59 seats although their vote did increase by 2.5 million: to this extent they were caught in the electoral trap of the third party.

Lloyd George was frustrated beyond measure. He complained that the new Prime Minister Ramsay MacDonald *lacked the driving energy which is essential in the emergency in which we stand.* He offered a deal. His Liberals, demonstrating daily in Parliament that they were the only party with a positive policy, would keep Labour in power if it brought in proportional representation. At the same time he schemed with an all-party group of young radicals, Oswald Mosley, Aneurin Bevan and Harold Macmillan, who admired his vision for the future. 'If Lloyd George had been able to form an administration, I do not think that any of the men who took part in these discussions would have refused to serve', wrote Oswald Mosley in his autobiography. Ll-G's former ally and fellow outsider Winston Churchill added his conspiratorial presence.

By the summer of 1931 Lloyd George seemed closer to regaining office than at any other time between 1922 and 1940. He was the man for the emergency and he was ready, as in 1916, to 'get things done'. MacDonald had no rescue remedy for the stagnant economy and the Labour Party depended on the Liberals for its survival. It is probable, though no firm evidence exists, that in July 1931 MacDonald offered Lloyd George a senior Government post, either the Foreign Office or the Treasury. At this crucial moment, 27 July, Ll-G was *hors de combat*, about to undergo an operation to remove his prostate gland. Over the next two months the stable political landscape of Britain was badly shaken and Lloyd George slid with it, from the heights of a possible national saviour to the depths of an isolated spectator. Seldom in politics can an illness have been worse-timed.

The day after his operation the Labour government reported a huge deficit of £120 million. It determined to save the economy by cutting unemployment relief by 10 per cent, although two million people were out of work and most of them were Labour voters. This split the Labour Cabinet down the middle so that it could no longer govern. It was Sir Herbert Samuel, Chairman of the Liberals, who suggested that the power vacuum should be filled by a National Government with MacDonald continuing as Prime Minister. Baldwin for the Conservatives agreed. This should have been the moment for Lloyd George to present himself as national saviour, and had he not been ill he would surely have played a decisive role. As it was he concurred from his sickbed and it was assumed he would take a government office as soon as he was fit.

In October MacDonald decided to call a general election. Ll-G opposed this on the predictable grounds that a national emergency was no time for party politics. Less predictably and certainly without evidence he saw it as a Conservative ploy to exploit the national crisis by advocating trade protection for purely party advantage. He spoke on the radio from Churt on

I have never seen a case of more complete disaster following so promptly on fatuous and pusillanimous leadership.

LLOYD GEORGE

15 October: *Under the guise of a patriotic appeal a Tory majority is to be engineered. Patriotism is everywhere exploited for purely party purposes.*[2] This conspiratorial view cost him credibility and power because he refused to join with the Liberals and support the National Government. It won a landslide victory in an election that saw the Labour Party divided in two, 13 MPs supporting the National Government and 52 opposing. The Liberal Party divided in three. In Lloyd George's absence an internecine squabble had continued between the Liberals under Lord Samuel who won 33 seats and the Liberal Nationalists under Lord Simon who won 35, though both supported the National Government. Standing outside, isolated and in a fit of pique, was a Welsh gang of four. These were Lloyd George's four Independent Liberals representing Welsh constituencies, his daughter Megan, his son Gwilym (who had been an MP since 1923) and Gwilym's brother in law – a minuscule family rump. It was a humiliation. He wrote to an old friend, Sir Herbert Lewis: *When I was stricken down in the late summer we had complete control of the Parliamentary situation. We had over 5,000,000 voters. Where are they now? I have never seen a case of more complete disaster following so promptly on fatuous and pusillanimous leadership.*[3] Now entering his 70th year it seemed the right time for Ll-G to retire to the orchards of Churt.

Chapter 6: The Elder Statesman (1931–45)

Lloyd George took his revenge writing five volumes of *War Memoirs*, castigating again the waste of trench warfare and arguing again his case for a more lateral strategy. His attack on Haig over Passchendaele was intended to wound: *The soldiers hardly ever caught a glimpse of their Commanders except when a vision of burnished brass flew past in a motor car. That is all they saw of the men who spoke the word that sent them to fight in the drowning mud.*[1] Based on much private material and full of insight, these *Memoirs* are compelling reading today.

In January 1935, on his 72nd birthday, Lloyd George announced Britain's 'New Deal'. Re-invigorated, and mindful that Gladstone had 15 years of politics ahead of him when he launched his Midlothian campaign aged 70, he called for a Council of Peace and Reconstruction to persuade the government to spend £2 million on public works and give wholehearted support to the League of Nations. He was taken sufficiently seriously for a Cabinet committee to consider his proposals and when Baldwin took over the premiership from MacDonald in June there were rumours that he might offer Lloyd George a seat in the Cabinet. With one eye on the imminent general election and the other on that Cabinet seat, Lloyd George let slip to Baldwin that unless the National Government took him seriously he had sufficient money left in his war chest to field 300 Liberal candidates who, at least, would increase Labour's chance of victory. This inducement misfired. The truth was that Lloyd George was seen more as a figure from the past than a radical innovator and there were plenty of radical Conservatives about, like Harold Macmillan, not to need this elder statesman getting in the way. Baldwin turned Lloyd George down and so did the electorate; only 21 Liberals were elected in November 1935. This time Baldwin had outwitted the Goat.

The following September, Lloyd George visited Adolf Hitler at his mountain retreat of Berchtesgaden. He was much flattered by Hitler's gift of a photo signed for 'the man who won the war' and said to his secretary, A J Sylvester, *Hitler is a great man. Führer is the proper name for him, for he is a born leader – yes, a statesman.* Lloyd George had been fascinated by the *Führer* ever since Hitler's rise to power in 1933 and he defended the aggressive way Hitler restored former territory to the Third Reich. He justified the Nazi re-occupation of the Rhineland (1936) and even the seizure of the German-speaking Sudetenland from Czechoslovakia after Munich (1938). To Ll-G both were predictable responses to the unfairness of the Treaty of Versailles and the refusal of France, in particular, to disarm. Hitler was only acting in self-defence. Ll-G wrote in the *Daily Express* after his return from Berchtesgaden: *the idea of a Germany intimidating Europe with a threat that its irresistible army might march across frontiers forms no part of his new vision.* This shows how fooled he was. Their mutual admiration did not just depend on flattery and a shared view of Versailles. Lloyd George liked the smack of firm government, particularly when it produced a programme of public works similar to the one he hoped to introduce in Britain. His utterances against fascism were mild though he called the Nazi persecution of the Jews *grave and deplor-*

able. He was also an admirer of the British Fascist Oswald Mosley.

Yet it would be wrong to call Lloyd George an appeaser. He disliked Mussolini as much as he admired Hitler and he argued for aiding the Republicans in the Spanish Civil War. When Germany invaded Poland in September 1939 and Britain declared war, he was all for bombing German munitions factories immediately. His views were somewhat schizophrenic but what united them was his belief in tough diplomacy: *There is no excuse at all for not taking strong action. The Government* [Neville Chamberlain's in 1938] *are behaving like a bevy of maiden aunts who have fallen among buccaneers. They just say 'Talk nicely to the gentlemen'. That is not the way to treat vital interests.*[2] The meek approach of Chamberlain's diplomacy infuriated Ll-G. It was reactive, not proactive, always seeking compromise, always outwitted by bullies. He considered that his own strong diplomacy allied to an understanding of Hitler would have averted war.

Hitler is a great man. Führer is the proper name for him, for he is a born leader – yes, a statesman.

LLOYD GEORGE

1940 was not Lloyd George's finest hour, but it was his final hour on the political stage. His attitude to the war maintained the ambivalence he had shown during the last years of peace. In his journalism he wrote defiantly against the Nazis; 'We Will Win Through' (*Sunday Pictorial* 21 July), and 'Hitler Cannot Frighten Us' (*Sunday Pictorial* 11 August). In private, and on one occasion in Parliament, he argued for a negotiated peace with Hitler. This was simple realism; he did not wish to sound defeatist but he could not see how Britain could survive on her own.

What offended him most was the irresolution, inactivity, of Chamberlain's government. In a devastating 20-minute speech in the House of Commons on 8 May he called for Chamberlain's resignation: *The nation is prepared for every sacrifice so long as it has leadership, so long as the Government show clearly what they are aiming at and so long as the nation is confident that those who are leading it are doing their best. I say solemnly that the Prime Minister should give an example of sacrifice, because there is nothing which can contribute more to victory than that he should sacrifice the seals of office.* Frances Stevenson was listening: 'There was still the same terrifying ring of scorn and anger in his voice. Chamberlain winced and wilted as the crushing blow descended upon him.' Other voices joined in.

I say solemnly that the Prime Minister should give an example of sacrifice, because there is nothing which can contribute more to victory than that he should sacrifice the seals of office.

LLOYD GEORGE

Two days later the German army invaded the Low Countries, Chamberlain resigned and Churchill became Prime Minister. Two weeks later the British Army retreated from Dunkirk. Now the tempo of change became so great and emotions under the surface so overwrought that Britons asked the unthinkable. Should they continue to defy Hitler? Seek peace terms? Surrender? Even stage some kind of revolution against the Tory 'appeasers' and 'blimps' (out-of-touch Generals) in order to produce a society that was worth fighting for and dying for? It was an extraordinary unstable summer; and the role of Lloyd George was in people's minds.

George Orwell wrote in his diary on 25 July: 'There are rumours that Lloyd George is the potential Pétain [the puppet ruler of Vichy France] of England. It is easy to imagine him playing this part but less easy to see him collaborating with the Tory clique who would be in favour of such a course.'[3] Possibly for this reason Churchill offered him a Cabinet post on 28 May; it was safer to have Ll-G in the Cabinet than

out as a focus of defeatists and peace-seekers. Lloyd George's reasons for refusing are significant: *we've got to get something like a revolution here and a better future for the common man. C & H* [Chamberlain and Lord Halifax, the Foreign Secretary, both appeasers still in the Cabinet] *don't want that. I do. Winston doesn't care either way. He will not smash the Tory Party to save the country, as I smashed the Liberal party* [in 1916].[4] This was an honourable reason for refusing.

There were many, however, who agreed with George Orwell: Ll-G was holding himself in reserve for such time as Britain was forced to negotiate. As an advocate of peace and an admirer of Hitler, he would be in a strong position. This says something about Lloyd George's untrustworthy reputation, yet if it was true it was a realistic position to take. Later that summer he changed his view to avoid the Pétain stigma. He still thought Britain was incapable of defeating Hitler on her own but considered negotiation from weakness not the answer: repel an invasion first and then negotiate from strength. In the end Churchill's inspiring leadership, Hitler's hesitation about ordering a full-scale invasion, and the simple patriotism of most Britons were enough to see out 1940 without any 'unthinkables' coming to pass.

In December Lloyd George turned down Churchill's final offer of the post of British Ambassador to the USA. He considered he was too old for the job and the Prime Minister agreed: 'I was conscious that he had aged even in the months that had passed since I had asked him to join the War Cabinet, and with regret but also with conviction I abandoned my plan.' What is remarkable is that Lloyd George was still seen as a man for the emergency, at 77, a quarter of a century after he had first filled that role.

On 20 January 1941 Dame Margaret Lloyd George died. Ll-G was badly shaken as well as distraught because he was prevented from being at her bedside by a snowstorm that trapped his car a few miles away. When his son Richard met him at Criccieth he found an old man weeping rather than the arch philanderer he expected to confront. Now Ll-G aged fast, appearing to shrink in every way except in the brightness of his eyes.

In May he made his last major parliamentary speech, a pessimistic one that goaded Churchill into a contemptuous reply: 'It was the sort of speech with which, I imagine, the illustrious and venerable Marshal Pétain might well have enlivened the closing days of M. Reynaud's Cabinet.' Lloyd George went home in a sulk and referred to himself sarcastically as *Old Papa Pétain*. Frances Stevenson was waiting for him. 'So Ll-G stayed at Churt, caring for his farm; or sitting in the big window, silent, for many days after Hitler attacked Russia, and what was going on in his mind I could not fathom.' He insisted on listening to 'Lord Haw Haw's' daily propaganda broadcasts from Germany that drove others at Churt out of the room. 'One day perhaps a psychiatrist will give an explanation of this,' wrote Frances Stevenson.

Two years later, on 23 October 1943, Ll-G and Frances Stevenson married at Guildford Registry Office. When Megan was told the previous evening she erupted: 'That woman!' and begged her father on the phone to call it off. Frances wrote: 'A deep contentment possessed me, but not the thrills of the usual bride. Our real marriage had taken place thirty years before.' The married couple spent a quiet year together before Ll-G was diagnosed as suffering from cancer. They returned for a holiday to the house of his childhood at Llanystumdwy, but it became clear that this was to be his resting place. 'One afternoon,' wrote Frances, 'when I thought he was asleep, he opened his eyes, turned to me, and said "Play 'Who will lead me to the strong City?'"' It was one of the Welsh hymns I had played him many times over the years at times of stress and trial.'[5]

The war was nearing its end and it became obvious that a general election was imminent. Lloyd George wanted to voice his opinion in Parliament against the policy of unconditional surrender and for a generous peace treaty, yet he was too ill to contest his safe seat of over half a century at Caernarvon Boroughs. Churchill thoughtfully offered him an earldom and in the New Year Honours List of 1945 he became Earl Lloyd-George of Dwyfor and Viscount Gwynedd. The press seemed less concerned that the People's David was now in the House of Lords than that Frances had been elevated from a secretary to a countess in 18 months. On 17 January the Earl Lloyd-George celebrated his 82nd birthday by walking round the village and retiring to read Charles Dickens. It was obvious that he was sinking quietly towards death. When it came on 26 March, Megan and Frances, only temporarily united, sat either side of his bed holding his hands. For one so eloquent there were no final words but seemingly a quiet contentment.

Lengthy obituaries that had been written long before now pasted him into the history books. Tributes 'poured in from all parts of the world', wrote Frances. Churchill, in Parliament, provided the formal peroration: 'When the British history of the first quarter of the 20th century is written, it will be seen how great a part of our fortunes in peace or in war were shaped by this one man.' It was another Welshman, Aneurin Bevan, who added a touch of poetry: 'We have lost in his death the most iridescent figure that ever illuminated the British political scene.'

Chapter 7: Lloyd George: An Assessment

Lloyd George and the Liberal Party

It has been said, most recently by historian Robert Skidelsky, that 'Lloyd George destroyed the Liberal Party'. Whichever way you look at the general election figures there seems dramatic evidence for this. In the great Liberal Government under Prime Minister Asquith 1910–16 there were over 270 Liberal MPs; then Lloyd George succeeded him, the Liberal Party split and with the single exception of 1923 it never succeeded in returning more than 68 MPs at any general election for the rest of the century. Specifically, Liberals have blamed Lloyd George for two dirty tricks. The first was the 'Coupon Election' of 1918 when he made a deal with the Conservatives to get his own Coalition Liberals into Parliament. The *Liberal Magazine* described it not unfairly thus: 'A prominent Liberal made a pact for joint action with the Conservatives, and conspired with the Conservative leaders to destroy every Liberal who refused to come into the deal.' The second was the building-up of his notorious Fund which he refused to share with the reunited Liberals at the 1923 and 1924 general elections. The virtually bankrupt Liberals lost heavily, so that Sydney Webb, husband of Beatrice, said he had witnessed 'the funeral of a great party'. Lady Asquith's incandescent letter to Baldwin in 1928 showed the fury of the Liberal faithful.

Yet both these actions were justified. In 1918 Asquith and his loyal Liberals refused to serve under Lloyd George who was, after all, the successful wartime Prime Minister. Asquith wrote: 'Under no conditions would I serve in a government of which Ll-G was head. I have learned by long & close association to mistrust him profoundly.' Understandably, Lloyd George did not wish to be taken hostage by the Conservatives so recruiting his own Coalition-supporting Liberals seemed the only answer.

After the war Lloyd George saw the Liberal establishment as worse than conservative, as fossilised. Asquith, he said, was *like a great boulder blocking the way. He could never form a government. There was no life in him.*[1] And it was true that Asquith had no new policies to fit the 1920s. That is why Lloyd George determined to found a new centre party and, after he failed, he waited until he succeeded Asquith to prepare the new Liberalism and spend his money wisely. The answer to the Liberal charge that Lloyd George destroyed the values of the party must be that he did his best to rescue the party from Asquith's gentlemanly inertia. His subsequent leadership of the Liberals proves this, for he evolved a completely new set of radical, probably workable, policies, and revived the party morale. Unfortunately the electorate in 1929 did not share his vision.

It is true that from about 1916 the Liberal Party was too small for both Asquith and Lloyd George. They conspired against each other and both must bear blame for the decline of the party. Yet Lloyd George did not commit the ultimate disloyalty. He did not stab Asquith in the back to become Prime Minister in 1916 or leader of the party in 1926. In

[Asquith was] *like a great boulder blocking the way. He could never form a government. There was no life in him.*
LLOYD GEORGE

1916 he wanted a free hand to run the war, which Asquith was incapable of doing, but he believed that power could be shared; that Asquith could remain as Prime Minister with him as Chairman of the War Council. Fortunately for Britain, Asquith rejected this compromise. However, Asquith's retirement into silence (unlike Neville Chamberlain in 1940 who loyally supported Churchill after he resigned from the premiership), encouraged the official Liberal Party to become an anti-Lloyd George faction. It was this that began its catastrophic decline. In 1923 Lloyd George returned to the fold as *a Liberal pure and simple* and served under Asquith, which says much for his order of priorities; *getting things done* was more important than party-political ambitions. Three years later it was Asquith's foolish dismissal of Lloyd George that led to his own resignation and to Ll-G becoming leader of the party.

Behind these squabbles over money and voting pacts were profound differences about the exercise of political power. To Asquith, his former Foreign Secretary Lord Grey and other Liberal elder statesmen, the exercise of power meant the persuasive but gentlemanly manipulation of like-minded colleagues who all respected the parliamentary system. They believed, too, that the Liberal Party embodied all that was honourable in British public life and maintaining this was an end in itself. Lloyd George was completely different. He saw himself as a man of the people. *The so-called Liberal Party,* he said in 1917, *consists mostly of plutocrats who have no sympathy whatever with the aspirations of the mass of people.* In fact, although his political beliefs were Liberal (see later) he was not really a party man. His tendency was to move towards the centre and establish a 'government of unity' as he proposed in 1910 and practised during the war. He had a creative drive *to get things done* and a preference for strong executive action over parliamentary procedure. As Prime Minister he believed he had the trust of the people. Given that, he was prepared to negotiate with sleight of hand, do deals with the Conservatives, hire 'captains of industry' to run government departments and behave in an illiberal way for what he saw as a Liberal end – the radical improvement in the lives of ordinary people. To Lloyd George the end justified the means; to Asquith it was the means that mattered.

This begs the question, could Lloyd George have saved the Liberal Party had he become undisputed leader after the war? The answer is surely no, for a reason unconnected with the Liberal Party in a narrow sense. Lloyd George's career in politics coincided with the rise in power of the Labour Party. Again, the general election figures tell their story. In 1900, the year of its birth (though it was not called the Labour Party until 1906), two Labour MPs were elected. In 1918 there were 63, in 1922 there were 142 and in 1929, when Labour formed its second government, there were 288. Considering that political configurations move slowly in British politics, the rise of the Labour Party was even more dramatic than the fall of the Liberal Party. Of course the two were connected and Liberal losses were Labour gains in the industrial heartlands of South Wales, the North of England and the Scottish lowlands. These years saw the rise of organised labour so that, as we have seen, over eight million workers belonged to trade unions and 6.5 million were affiliated to the Trades Union Congress, an integral part of the Labour movement. Trade union power increased and that of the Dissenting chapel, a focus for Liberal politics when Lloyd George began his career, declined. In a way socialism was the new religion.

Political parties in Britain are based on class and after the war Labour became the authentic party of the working class, whether those who voted for it were socialists or not. They remained loyal to it even in 1929, when Lloyd George offered a Liberal manifesto that was far more positive in coping with the Depression than the Labour alternative. The last era when the Liberal party was able to offer a social reforming but non-socialist manifesto that attracted working-class support was during the pre-war Asquith government.

The Liberal Party, then, was undermined as a party of power more by the rise of the Labour Party than the machinations of Lloyd George and Asquith. But the machinations of Baldwin and MacDonald were relevant too. Both men hated and feared Lloyd George and liked each other. There was an understanding between them, long before they shared power in the National Government of 1931, that Lloyd George should be removed as a rival. Leo Amery spoke for his boss Baldwin in 1923: 'The real health and natural division of parties is between constructive Conservatism and Labour Socialism. It is in the interests of both to clear the ground of the Liberal Party ... We may each hope to get a larger share of the carcass but the great thing is to get the beast killed.'[2] From the Labour side, Ramsay MacDonald told the editor of *The Guardian* in 1924 that 'he could get on with the Tories, but the Liberals were cads'. In the 1920s this animosity stood in the way of any further re-alignment of Liberals with either Conservative or Labour parties and in the general elections between the wars the Liberals were squeezed between the other two parties. It is possible that if Lloyd George had enacted some form of proportional representation legislation as part of the 1918 Representation of the People Act, and the opportunity existed, then the Liberal Party might have shared power in 1929. This was its big opportunity. As it was, only 59 Liberal MPs were elected although the party won almost 30 per cent of the vote. For this it is fair to place some blame on Lloyd George.

From the time he became Prime Minister, Lloyd George's enemies within the Liberal Party and without said that he was not a true Liberal at all; that he had forsaken the party's policies and traditions for the devious pursuit of power. Was he a true Liberal? Certainly, no one would have asked that question of the Boy David. He came to prominence as an MP because he campaigned for the causes of Gladstonian Liberalism – Free Trade, Home Rule (for Ireland, Wales and the Boers in South Africa), the disestablishment of the church and teetotalism. These were the late 19th century Liberal beliefs in individualism and liberty with a strong chapel influence added. No one questioned the Liberalism of the People's David either. As Chancellor of the Exchequer he transformed the traditional Liberalism by adding his social programme of pensions and national insurance based on a new, redistributive, fiscal policy. This new dimension of social concern that was not socialist wrested the initiative from the Conservative and Labour Parties while being consistent with old Liberal values.

It was during the war that Lloyd George's critics began to question his Liberal credentials. For many the test case was conscription, and forcing men to fight is certainly an illiberal measure. Then there was the central direction of the war effort with strong elements of compulsion represented by DORA – the Defence of the Realm Act. After the war the Prime Minister's strong-arm tactics in dealing with the IRA by hiring the 'Black and Tans' and with striking workers by the Emergency Powers Act similarly offended Liberal sensitivities. The 'Geddes Axe' of 1922 seemed to confirm that he was a leader without Liberal sympathies. Yet were it not for his suspect lifestyle and Conservative associates, together with his scheming to build a party within the party, then these illiberal measures might surely have been excused as strong executive action forced on the Prime Minister by war, international and civil. In any event Lloyd George defended his record robustly, writing to C P Scott of *The Guardian* just after his resignation: *I cannot accept that I am a traitor to Liberalism. As a matter of fact the record of Liberal measures is a fine one – the greatest measure of Irish self-government, a very great measure of franchise extension, a not insignificant measure of land reform, a remarkable temperance measure, an important international agreement as to disarmament.*[3]

After the war the old Gladstonian Liberalism lost its relevance and Lloyd George was soon working on a new agenda; the Green, Yellow and Orange policies. Although the term neo-Liberalism is most often used in relation to the New Deal in the United States, it stands for the acceptance of the state as an instrument to reduce economic inequalities and therefore to empower the individual. Lloyd George's neo-Liberalism added economic justice to the social concerns of the great Liberal reforms before the war and may be seen as a further extension of Gladstone's urge for a more democratic society. The term 'orange' is sometimes used to describe Liberal policies today.

I cannot accept that I am a traitor to Liberalism.

LLOYD GEORGE

Assessing the Liberal career of Lloyd George over his full 55 years as an MP, one consistently radical, indeed revolutionary, policy stands out; this is his unswerving commitment to land reform, to the redistribution of the ownership of land. His root-and-branch vendetta against big landowners amounted to an attack on the House of Lords, on the British class system, on the very definition of what it meant to be British.

In one of his first major speeches at Bangor in 1891, he used an historical argument: *The land of this country was distributed amongst its owners, the predecessors of the present owners, for the express purpose of enabling them to defend the country. The land was also to maintain royalty, and to bear the expense of dispensing justice and preserving law and order. Now what has happened? The land is still in the possession of a privileged few, but what has become of the burden of maintaining the army, law, order and royalty? It has been shifted onto the shoulders of the toilers of this country. This must be equalised. This deplorable state of things cannot go on.*[4] Almost exactly 50 years later, in his last important speech in the House of Commons, he argued for the nationalisation of land: *Let the Government go in for a bold, comprehensive, far-reaching policy and demand that the resources of the nation be put behind it, as it can be. Then if there is a victory for the battle of freedom, independence and right, the soil of England has shared the credit.*[5] To Ll-G *Back to the land!* was the panacea for the nation's ills. However much his Liberal philosophy may have wavered or changed, he remained true to his core belief that land reform was needed for a more democratic and free society.

Lloyd George's 'people's budget' of 1909 was his first legislative attack on the big landowners. As we have seen, it offended them because he proposed one tax on the 'unearned increment' of land values and a second on the capital value of underdeveloped land. When the House of Lords threw out the budget, he made a number of speeches remarkable for their ferocity, such as this mob oratory in Newcastle on 8 October: *Who made ten thousand people owners of the soil? Who made the rest of us trespassers in the land of our birth? Who is responsible for the scheme of things whereby one man is engaged through life in grinding labour and another man receives without toil every hour of the day, every hour of the night when he slumbers, more than his neighbour receives in a whole year of toil?*[6]

There is no denying Ll-G's sincerity nor the injustice that he railed against. In 1913 he began a Land Campaign *to emancipate the land in this country from the paralysing grip of a rusty, effete and unprofitable system. The land is the greatest, the most essential, of our national assets.* With his usual energy he commissioned a vast Rural Report. Based on this he made a number of recommendations that eventually were part of the Corn Production Bill of 1917 (see above), but the sting was in the tail: *the present system of rating, insofar as it discourages improvement by either owner or cultivator, and rewards the indolent who declines to put his land to the best use, must be reconsidered and recast.* Lloyd George's determination to reward the small farmer for his husbandry and penalise the indolent landowner was to become the controversial and revolutionary recommendation of his 'green book', *The Land and the Nation*, published in 1925. He launched it at a massive rally in Devon on 17 September when he spoke for an hour and a half to a crowd of 25,000 standing in the rain without, it was reported, losing a single person.

Who made ten thousand people owners of the soil? Who made the rest of us trespassers in the land of our birth?

LLOYD GEORGE

He proposed the notion of 'cultivating tenure'. From an 'appointed date' all cultivatable land would be taken over by the state which would assess how well it was being farmed. If necessary, having paid compensation to the previous owner, the state would then transfer the land *to any person competent to use it to the advantage of the community as a whole.*[7] The new tenant would be encouraged to farm it for profit; he would benefit from state aid and be able to leave the tenancy to his heir but he was not allowed to sell it. A more revolutionary change can scarcely be imagined in peacetime – a transfer of estates owned sometimes by the same family for hundreds of years into quasi-nationalisation. Asquith and other Liberal elders were scandalised. Lloyd George was forced to water down his proposals, but they showed where his heart lay. He was a rural radical who never forgot the injustices caused by land ownership in the North Wales of his youth. From first to last he championed the individual small farmer and disliked the social, semi-feudal aristocracy that was based on the land.

Does this make him a Liberal or a socialist? He was quite clear about this, writing in 1926: *I am not a Socialist, but a Liberal. I believe that the elimination of private enterprise and individual incentive will be a disaster to the well being of the country. I have only advocated public ownership when private enterprise has conspicuously broken down or proved itself inadequate to public needs.*[8]

At the same time, Ll-G's beliefs were also a long way from the self-help and rugged individualism of the Victorian Liberal ethic. From the 'people's budget' of 1909 onwards he used the state as a social engine to improve people's lives. When he set up the Ministry of Munitions in 1915 and provided housing, good food and even factory cinemas for the workers, he hailed *the new ideas that are abroad. Employers and workers, the public and the state, are all favourable to new methods. The effort now being made to secure the welfare of the workers will leave behind results of enduring value.* He was right. In Tony Blair's seminal lecture to the Fabian Society in 1995, *Let Us Face the Future*, in which he laid out the ground for New Labour, he praised the New Liberalism of Lloyd George: 'The New Liberals were both liberals with a small "l" and social democrats, living on the cusp of a new age ... Their intellectual energy drove the 1910 government that legislated for improved working conditions, an embryonic welfare system and progressive taxation. They recognised that socially created wealth could legitimately be used for social purposes, even if this required changes in the existing order of property rights ... It was a credo of social reform and state action to emancipate individuals from the vagaries and oppressions of personal circumstances … Democratic socialism in Britain was indeed the political heir of the radical Liberal tradition.'[9]

Lloyd George was all for harnessing the power of the state to improve the well-being of its workers but he mistrusted trade unions and socialism. This was not just ideological. He was deeply suspicious of Bolshevism and used the sort of language more associated with Churchill who spoke of 'plague-bearing Russia'. Ll-G once said: *Syndicalism* [a belief that trade unions should take over the state] *and Socialism are two completely different things. They are mutually destructive and there is this guarantee for society that one microbe can be trusted to kill another.*

In his restless pursuit of power in the 1920s, Lloyd George schemed with both Conservative and Labour politicians in his quest for a middle ground; and he cut ground from under the Liberals. But there was no doubt where his political prejudices lay. He said in 1924: *Toryism would confiscate, in the interests of private monopoly, the produce of industry, the toil, the capital, the risk and effort of others. Socialism would also confiscate, in the interests of state monopoly, the efforts of the individual.* In 1925, at a time when totalitarianism was taking root in Europe in the aftermath of the war, he accused both Conservative and Labour parties of potential tyranny. *Scratch a Conservative and you find a Fascist*, he said and a month later he said of socialism: *It is like the sands of the desert. It gets into your food, your clothes, your machinery, the very air you breathe. They are all gritty with regulations, orders, decrees, rules.* The *sanely progressive* Liberal Party stood in between these two dangerous forces. *Liberalism stands between two confiscatory systems for a free opportunity for the individual to do the best for himself and the nation.*[10]

Lloyd George as Prime Minister

Although Lloyd George was voted in a millennium poll of historians as second only to Churchill as the outstanding prime minister of the 20th century, his reputation since the early 1920s has been badly tarnished by the notoriety of his private life. Had he retired from politics in 1918 as 'the man who won the war' and founded the welfare state, he would doubtless be regarded today as one of our greatest leaders. Instead, mention of Lloyd George provokes gossip about his promiscuous sex life, the meaningful recitation of the music-hall ditty 'Lloyd George knew my father, my father knew Lloyd George' with the implication that the next line goes something like 'and that's why he bought an honour' (though neither the origin nor the meaning of the song are known) or the expostulation (from an elderly Welsh Conservative in this case) 'Lloyd George? He was nothing but a liar and a thief!'

A J P Taylor wrote that Lloyd George's premiership 'was dynamic and sordid at the same time'. He makes his case with a journalist's relish and a historian's references. Lloyd George's attitude to money was careless and self-serving so that he was 'the first prime minister since Horace Walpole to leave office flagrantly richer than when he entered it'. His private life was 'irregular' so that he was also 'the first prime minister since the Duke of Grafton to live openly with his mistress'. He could have added that Lloyd George's attitude to the honours system was cynical and crude. He did add that 'he had no friends and did not deserve any'. Taylor attributes all this to Ll-G's devious nature, quoting out of context surely the line from *War Memoirs*: *I never believed in costly frontal attacks either in war or politics, if there was a way round.*[11]

A strong defence may be mounted of Lloyd George. Perhaps it is a euphemism to say that 'a Scotsman's truth is a straight line, a Welshman's is more or less a curve', but

Ll-G's manipulative manner and 'way round' that was economical with the truth – very effective in negotiations – had another side – extraordinary eloquence. An old friend, and Ll-G did have a faithful group of friends, wrote in 1939: 'he has always possessed that indefinable thing which we call eloquence – the power of saying things in such a way as to make them felt in the innermost recesses of one's being.' Many times he held vast crowds, or a crowded House of Commons, in the palms of his hands; inspiring a nation (his speech in the Queen's Hall, London, in September 1914), demolishing a reputation (Neville Chamberlain's in May 1940), or winning round a sceptical audience (the Maurice debate in May 1918). He loved neither honours nor money for their own sake but simply for the necessary power they gave him. That is why he was so blatant and careless in their dispensation and acquisition.

As for his relationships, certainly Lloyd George took loyal service for granted and did not allow personal friendships to stand in the way of public duty, but that is a quality. He was a superb judge of character, his empathy once again, and in nearly every case his headhunting in the war was successful, from captains of industry like Sir Joseph Maclay to academics like H A L Fisher. The picture of Ll-G as a rootless and heartless emigrant from Wales who abandoned his wife and family in order to live a newly-rich lifestyle in the Home Counties with his mistress is far from accurate. His attachment was always to Wales, the Welsh language, the National Eisteddfod (which he always attended), hymn-singing round the hearth or in chapel. Promiscuous he certainly was but for most of his adult life he loved two women and they loved him.

More important was what A J P Taylor called the 'dynamism' of Lloyd George's rule. He goes on to compare him with Napoleon, 'a supreme ruler maintaining himself by individual achievement'. 'Volatile genius' is the phrase used by another historian, Kenneth Morgan. From the time he took office Lloyd George, now sometimes called 'the Big Beast of the Forest' as well as 'the Goat', overthrew traditional processes. He established a new form of cabinet government and used his own advisers; he set up new government departments run by new men from outside politics; he controlled these in new ways in which the planning, monitoring and targeting resembled a form of war socialism. He set up what Morgan called 'a new leviathan of state power'. He was everywhere, a sort of one man Minister-of-All-Departments. Partly this was forced on Lloyd George because he had no party behind him and he was an outsider. Partly it was because he was good at this form of 'ad hoc' intervention; he had the creative energy, the determination, the agility and the necessary lack of scruple. Britain had a war to win.

The truth was that he preferred this style of government. It played to his strengths and his inclinations. His biggest paradox was that he was an instinctive democrat but a natural autocrat. He chose the company of like-minded strong executives from industry and he admired presidential-style rulers abroad, both the Roosevelts in the United States and Hitler. He was not a political philosopher, though he had deep-felt political beliefs, but a man of action. He had shown his preference for this kind of strong executive rule free from party politics in his famous Memorandum on Forming a Coalition of 1910. Significantly, only Winston Churchill shared his enthusiasm.

The tragedy was that Lloyd George's political style predisposed a different political world. Government in Britain is in the hands of political parties that are represented in a strong legislature. From this the executive Cabinet is chosen and power is dispensed according to the principle of collective responsibility and accountability. Lloyd George would have thrived in a system of shifting interest-groups coalescing round different causes rather than permanent parties. He would have preferred a strong executive chosen from all talents, much as he had in his War Cabinet. As Morgan said 'the volatile genius of one man was in conflict with the conservative mould of a conservative country'.[12] During the war the country accepted his 'Napoleonic' government but in peacetime people wanted, in Baldwin's words, a return to normality and the end of 'that dynamic force'.

Much has been written about Lloyd George's qualities of leadership. John Grigg's view, after spending nearly 30 years on his biography, was that 'Lloyd George was a political genius in whom the qualities of crusader, adventurer and rogue bewilderingly co-existed'.[13] However, what makes him such an attractive figure is his love of life, bubbling to the surface whatever the grim realities lurking below. In *War Memoirs* he describes a drive near Cannes with Bonar Law, before the Great War: *The sky was cloudless and the sea was blue as only the Mediterranean can be. I turned to Bonar Law and asked him if he did not think it beautiful. 'I don't care much for scenery' he replied in his rather toneless voice. The night before I had been to a performance of one of Mozart's operas – I think it was 'Il Seraglio' – and I was struck by its exquisite beauty. I mentioned the fact to Bonar Law, but his reaction to my enthusiasm was only to say 'I don't care much for music'. As we approached a golf course we saw some extremely pretty women. I called Bonar Law's attention to them. 'Women don't attract me' was his laconic answer. 'Will you tell me what', I said exasperated at this disdain for the attractions of life, 'what it is that you do care for? Scenery – music – women – none of them has any meaning for you.' 'I like bridge' was the reply.*[14]

Lloyd George may well have made a more popular prime

minister today than most of his successors. His witty one-liners, his lack of pomposity and classless image, his love of the limelight and intuitive empathy with his audiences, would have made him a TV star. This is a less hierarchical and deferential age than the 1920s. It would have suited his style.

A comparison can well be made between the premierships of David Lloyd George and Tony Blair, as much in their styles of leadership as in their politics. Lloyd George was accused of disregarding the British constitution by his personal, quasi-presidential style of government and so is Blair with his 'sofa politics'. In terms of management, both relied on their own advisers (the Garden Suburb set in Ll-G's time) at the expense of government departments, particularly the Foreign Office. Neither had much time for Cabinet government, nor attended Parliament more than was strictly necessary. Both employed secretaries who became notorious for their use of 'spin' (Sir William 'Bronco Bill' Sutherland was Ll-G's press secretary) and for twisting the arms of backbenchers (Captain Freddie Guest was Ll-G's Chief Whip). In terms of diplomacy, both were highly interventionist, preferring the big picture to sorting out the detail, grandstanding round the globe taking bold initiatives and expecting that others would look after the implementation. Both were amazingly quick at understanding an issue, more adept at face-to-face briefing than the quiet study of documents. In terms of day-to-day politics, both were political seducers of great charm and effect and neither was very trustworthy when it came to remembering exactly what was agreed. Both were very effective speechmakers, partly because they made the most of their accessibility and seeming classlessness. Neither of them was a loyal party politician because both occupied the middle ground and saw themselves as custodians of social democracy rather than of a party tradition: New Liberal, New Labour. Both were energetic, effective, and stayed on too long for the good of their reputations.

In 1917, Lloyd George's friend Sir George Riddell wrote this assessment of the Prime Minister's qualities and defects: 'His energy, capacity for work, and power of recuperation are remarkable. He has an extraordinary memory, imagination, and the art of getting at the root of a matter. He is not afraid of responsibility, and has no respect for tradition or convention. He is always ready to examine, scrap, or revise established theories and practices. These qualities give him unlimited confidence in himself. He is one of the craftiest of men, and his charm of manner not only wins him friends, but does much to soften the asperities of opponents. He is full of humour and a born actor. He has an instinctive power of divining the intentions of people with whom he is conversing. His chief defects are: (1) Lack of appreciation of existing institutions. (2) Fondness for a grandiose scheme in preference to an attempt to improve existing machinery. (3) Disregard of difficulties in carrying out big projects. He is not a man of detail.'[15]

Would an assessment of Prime Minister Blair be very different?

Lloyd George was christened 'the man who won the war' because that was the popular verdict at the time. After the armistice he was given an unprecedented standing ovation in the House of Commons. Honours were showered on him, the Order of Merit from the King, the Grand Cordon of the Legion d'Honneur in France, the freedom of cities. That verdict stands today. He was the only senior member of the government with the will to win, the drive and energy, the vision and inspiration, the indomitable spirit. The two Tory Prime Ministers past and future, Balfour and Bonar Law, perceived this in 1916. They stood aside and encouraged Lloyd George to become Prime Minister, although they shared neither his political principles nor his dictatorial style. 'Let him be', said Balfour. 'If he thinks he can win the war, I'm all for his having a try'.

The new Prime Minister, typically, did not think he had enough power: *The President of the United States is a Dictator for four years. He can do practically as he pleases. If I were in that position I could accomplish many things which are now impossible or which can only be accomplished by endless manoeuvring.* This may read as hubris but more likely it stemmed from frustration. In any event a truer insight into Ll-G's mind at the time comes from his own description in *War Memoirs*. Here was the man ultimately responsible for meeting the challenge of the most destructive war in history: *What must be the sensation of a man who took a leading part in the direction of this tremendous war and undertakes to recall these events with their horrors, their perils and their amazing escapes? It is like a traveller who revisits dangerous rapids through which he once tried to navigate without a map, without knowledge, and without experience to guide him or any of the crew as to the course of the river, its depths and its shallows, its sharp and unexpected bends, the strengths and whirl of the current, · or the location of hidden rocks in its channel.*[16]

In fact it is clear that Lloyd George made two massive contributions that plucked victory out of the jaws of defeat. In the first place he transformed Britain into a nation at war. He began this before he became Prime Minister by creating the Ministry of Munitions. He continued as soon as he became Prime Minister by setting up a professionally-run, constantly meeting War Cabinet. Then came other new ministries, of

Food, of Shipping, of Labour, and a mass of legislation about conscription, labour relations, pricing and profits that pushed a democratic society as far as it could go. He galvanised the nation's effort by his 'war socialism', his inspirational speeches and his interventionist drive. In the end he was the man who supplied the guns, the ammunition and the shipping that won the war.

In the second place he intervened at two crucial times in the war when defeat was quite possible. In 1916 Germany was confident that it would starve Britain into surrender and top advice to Lloyd George did not dissent from this. His answer was to drive towards self-sufficiency in food and to introduce a system of rationing. It was also to force on the reactionary Admiralty the introduction of the convoy system. Both interventions were decisive. In the spring of 1918 the Ludendorff offensive broke through the Allied lines on the Western Front and Lloyd George acted when others seemed paralysed. He successfully persuaded President Wilson to commit American troops to the fighting and he encouraged Haig to counterattack by the supply of fresh troops that nearly equalled the number of those captured, killed or wounded (200,000). Once again his intervention was decisive.

Lloyd George was constantly irritated and undermined by his most senior generals. He must share the blame for this. He lacked his customary empathy with them and he did little to rectify it. Moreover, he cannot be absolved from the disaster of Passchendaele. At the end of the day Lloyd George consented to the offensive of Third Ypres and he did not order Haig to abandon it. Haig, who for all his faults was a political democrat, would have obeyed. Yet Lloyd George did break up the obstructive duo of Haig and Robertson and he did set up the Supreme War Council. In 1918 he also obtained the appointment of Foch as the 'Generalissimo' instead of Haig, ironically not long before Haig launched his last offensive that was for once well planned and co-ordinated.

Compared to the Western Front all the other theatres of Britain's war were sideshows. This was Lloyd George's enduring complaint. Yet Allenby's campaign against the Turks in Palestine and the Middle East destroyed the Ottoman Empire. It provided a huge boost to morale in the winter of 1917 and its effect on global politics today gives it a huge significance that it did not have at the time. This was very much Lloyd George's triumph achieved in spite of the military establishment. No wonder Allenby said 'the Little Man won the war'.

Lloyd George was also the Prime Minister who made the peace. He was the only statesman to survive in office from the first settlement to the last and the only one of the Big Four at Versailles with the energy and staying power to really grapple with the issues. 'He is fighting like a terrier, all by himself', said a British diplomat of Lloyd George's attempts to get Germany a fairer deal. T E Lawrence, who left the peace conferences disillusioned, nevertheless said of him: 'He is head and shoulders above anyone else ... The only man there in a big position who was really trying to do what was right.' He was a maker of the modern world, for better or worse. No other British prime minister with the exception of Churchill had such an impact. If the Second World War was a continuation of the First World War because of the punitive Treaty of Versailles, then Lloyd George was partly responsible for this; but he also realised that it would provoke Germany into retaliation and he tried to undo its harshest measures. When he returned with 'an honourable peace' he added later *but we shall have to do the whole thing over again in twenty-five years at three times the cost*.

Today's Balkan politics is a new attempt to achieve what Lloyd George and his fellow peacemakers initiated – the self-

determination of small nations. Today's destructive confrontation between Jews and Arabs in the former Palestine began as a well meaning attempt by Lloyd George, Balfour and others to satisfy the national aspirations of two opposed peoples. He was more successful with devolution than self-determination. He made sure that Wales was treated as a political reality and his Irish Free State treaty was the foundation of today's Ireland, north and south.

Boundaries, constitutions, treaties, all affect indirectly how people live their lives. Lloyd George's radical domestic legislation affected directly the lives of the British people more than the legislation of any other modern prime minister including Churchill. He launched the welfare state, he introduced the 'war socialism' repeated in the next war and he pioneered the 'middle way' of social democracy. What this meant in terms of family life in 1919, although there were many exceptions, was that the grandparents could receive a state pension, the father could claim from the state unemployment and sickness benefit, and the mother could well be in work. They could all vote. Their children would stay at school until they were 14 and sit a state exam. That year at least the family would benefit from food rationing but find drinking hours at the pub restricted. But Britain was not the land that Lloyd George had promised, 'a land fit for heroes to live in.' He had no answer to the mounting debts of war nor to the Depression that followed soon afterwards.

The achievements of Prime Minister David Lloyd George, the adopted nephew of a Welsh shoemaker, were huge. But his subsequent life was a political tragedy. He was brought down at the height of his powers, partly because of the way he used these powers. But for such a genius on the national stage his protracted demise through the 1920s and 1930s was such a waste, for him and for Britain.

NOTES

Introduction

1. J M Keynes, *Essays in Biography* (London: 1933) pp 36–7.
2. Francis Lloyd George, *The Years That Are Past* (Hutchinson, London: 1967) pp 40–2.
3. Quoted by Peter Rowland, *David Lloyd George* (Macmillan, New York: 1976) p 748.

Chapter 1: The Boy David (1863–1905)

1. Quoted by John Grigg, *The Young Lloyd George* (Penguin, London: 1997) p 44.
2. Quoted by Grigg, *The Young Lloyd George*, p 49.
3. Quoted by Rowland, *David Lloyd George*, p 48.
4. Quoted by Grigg, *The Young Lloyd George*, p 67
5. Quoted Rowland, David Lloyd George, pp 68–9.
6. *Manchester Guardian*, 1900.
7. Walter Davies of Criccieth, quoted by Rowland, *David Lloyd George*, p 146.

Chapter 2: The People's David (1905–16)

1. Quote by John Grigg, *The People's Champion 1902–1911* (Penguin, London: 1997) p 113.
2. Quoted by Grigg, *The People's Champion*, p 156
3. Quoted by Rowland, *David Lloyd George*, p 260.
4. *The Diary of Beatrice Webb* Vol 3, 1905–1924 (London, Virago: 1984) p 149.
5. Quoted by Kenneth Morgan, *The Age of Lloyd George* (Allen & Unwin: 1978) p 150.

6. Quoted by John Grigg, *From Peace to War 1912 – 1916* (Penguin, London: 1997) pp 164–5.

7. David Lloyd George, *War Memoirs* Vol 1 (Odhams Press, London: 1938) pp 220, 235–8, hereafter *War Memoirs* 1.

8. Frances Lloyd George, *The Years That Are Passed*, p 72.

9. Quoted by Frances Lloyd George, *The Years That Are Passed*, pp 88–9.

10. Quoted by Frances Lloyd George, *The Years That Are Passed*, p 89.

11. *War Memoirs* 1, pp 602–3.

Chapter 3: The Man Who Won The War (1916–18)

1. *War Memoirs* 1, p 621.

2. *War Memoirs* 1, p 612.

3. *The Diary of Beatrice Webb* Vol 3, 9 Dec. 1916, p 272.

4. Lord Esher, quoted by Rowland, *David Lloyd George*, p 382.

5. *War Memoirs* 1, p 619.

6. *War Memoirs* 1, p 667.

7. *The Diary of Beatrice Webb* Vol 3, March 1917, p 276.

8. A J P Taylor, *The First World War* (Penguin, London: 1966) p 194.

9. Quoted by Grigg, *From Peace to War*, p 377.

10. Frances Stevenson, *Lloyd George, A Diary* (edited by A J P Taylor, London: 1971) pp 92–3.

11. David Lloyd George, *War Memoirs* Vol 2 (Odhams Press, London: 1936), pp 2014–5, hereafter *War Memoirs* 2.

12. WPC minutes, 21 June 1917.

13. *War Memoirs* 2, p 1370.

14. Both quotes by John Grigg, *War Leader 1916 – 1918* (Penguin, London: 2003) pp 449–50.

15. Harold Nicholson, quoted by Rowland, *David Lloyd George* p 460.

Chapter 4: The Man Who Made The Peace (1918–22)

1. Margaret MacMillan, *Peacemakers* (John Murray, London: 2001) p 62.
2. Quoted by MacMillan, *Peacemakers*, p 392.
3. Quoted by Morgan, *The Age of Lloyd George*, p 198.
4. Quoted by Grigg, *War Leader 1916–1918*, pp 117–18.
5. Quoted by Peter Rowland, *David Lloyd George*, p 568.

Chapter 5: The Leader in Waiting (1922–31)

1. *The Diary of Beatrice Webb* Vol 3, March 1918, p 299.
2. Quoted by John Campbell, *Lloyd George, The Goat in the Wilderness* (Jonathan Cape, London: 1977) p 302.
3. Quoted by Rowland, *David Lloyd George*, p 695.

Chapter 6: The Elder Statesman 1931–45

1. For Ll-G's diatribe against Haig see *War Memoirs* Vol 2, pp 2011–31.
2. Quoted by Rowland, *David Lloyd George*, p 743.
3. George Orwell, *Collected Essays and Letters* (Penguin, London: 1970), *Wartime Diary* p 412.
4. Ll-G to his former assistant Tom Jones, quoted by Rowland, *David Lloyd George*, p 776.
5. All these quotes from Frances Lloyd George, *The Days That Are Passed*, pp 268–78.

Chapter 7: Lloyd George: An Assessment

1. Quoted by Campbell, *Lloyd George, The Goat in the Wilderness*, pp 54–5.
2. Quoted by Campbell, *Lloyd George, The Goat in the Wilderness*, p 87n.
3. Quoted by Rowland, *David Lloyd George*, p 585.
4. Quoted by Grigg, *The Young Lloyd George*, pp 112–13.
5. Quoted by Rowland, *David Lloyd George*, p 784.

6. Quoted by Grigg, *The People's Champion*, pp 204–15, 225.

7. For policy document see Morgan, *The Age of Lloyd George*, pp 214–16.

8. Quoted by Rowland, *David Lloyd George*, p 628

9. Tony Blair, *Let Us Face The Future*, Fabian pamphlet 571, 1995.

10. Quoted by Campbell, *Lloyd George, The Goat in the Wilderness*, pp 108–9.

11. A J P Taylor, *English History 1914–1945* (Penguin, London: 1975) pp 109–11.

12. Kenneth Morgan, *George, David Lloyd*, in *Dictionary of National Biography,* pp 909–11.

13. Grigg, *The Young Lloyd George*, p 13.

14. *War Memoirs* 1, p 614.

15. Quoted by Grigg, *War Leader 1916–1918*, pp 220–1.

16. *War Memoirs* 1, p 667.

CHRONOLOGY

Year	Premiership

1916 Lloyd George, Secretary of State for War, dismayed by Asquith's handling of the war, forms alliance with Bonar Law and Balfour, and suggests a small War Cabinet with him as chairman; Asquith refuses, Lloyd George and Bonar Law threaten resignation.

6 December: Barely a month before his 54th birthday, Lloyd George becomes Prime Minister. He forms War Cabinet, including Balfour, Curzon, Milner, Henderson

1917 Lloyd George forces Admiralty to accept convoy system and sets up new Ministries of Food and of Shipping. He fails to prevent tragedy of Passchendaele (Third Ypres) but is delighted by capture of Jerusalem. His Cabinet announces the Balfour Declaration favouring the establishment of a national home for the Jewish People in Palestine.

1918 Lloyd George persuades the French to appoint Foch supreme Allied commander on the Western Front and sacks the CIGS, Robertson. He imposes martial law in Ireland. He supplies fresh troops to meet Ludendorff's Spring Offensive and defends his record in the Maurice debate in May. He oversees Education Act and Representation of the People Act. In August Haig launches massive offensive and in November Germany surrenders. Lloyd George receives Order of Merit and is hailed as 'the man who won the war'. In December he wins massive majority (262 seats) in the general ('coupon') election for the continuation of the Coalition Government.

History	Culture
First World War. Western Front: Battle of Verdun, France. Battle of the Somme, France. US President Woodrow Wilson is re-elected. US President Wilson issues Peace Note to belligerents in European war. Development and use of first effective tanks.	Lionel Curtis, *The Commonwealth of Nations.* James Joyce, *Portrait of an Artist as a Young Man.* Max Brod, *Tycho Brahe's Weg zu Gott.* Vicente Blasco Ibanez, *The Four Horsemen of the Apocalypse.* Matisse, *The Three Sisters.* Monet, *Waterlilies.* 'Dada' movement produces iconoclastic 'anti-art'. Richard Strauss, *Ariadne auf Naxos.* Ethel Smythe, *The Boatswain's Mate.* Film: *Intolerance.*
First World War. February Revolution in Russia. USA declares war on Germany. China declares war on Germany and Russia. German and Russian delegates sign armistice at Brest-Litovsk.	P G Wodehouse, *The Man With Two Left Feet.* T S Eliot, *Prufrock and Other Observations.* Leon Feuchtwanger, *Jud Suess.* Piet Mondrian launches *De Stijl* magazine in Holland. Picasso designs 'surrealist' costumes and set for Satie's *Parade.* Hans Pfitzner, *Palestrina.* Prokofiev, *Classical Symphony.* Film: *Easy Street.*
First World War. Peace Treaty of Brest-Litovsk between Russia and the Central Powers. Romania signs Peace of Bucharest with Germany and Austria-Hungary. Ex-Tsar Nicholas II and family executed. German Chancellor Hertling resigns. Armistice signed between Allies and Germany; German Fleet surrenders. Kaiser Wilhelm II of German abdicates.	Alexander Blok, *The Twelve.* Gerald Manley Hopkins, *Poems.* Luigi Pirandello, *Six Characters in Search of an Author.* Bela Bartok, *Bluebeard's Castle.* Puccini, *Il Trittico.* Gustav Cassel, *Theory of Social Economy.* Kokoshka, *Friends* and *Saxonian Landscape.* Edvard Munch, *Bathing Man.*

1919   Lloyd George attends Peace Conference in Paris in January
and returns with Treaty of Versailles in June. He passes the
Emergency Powers Act to deal with industrial unrest and sets
up the Sankey commission on the coalmines. In October he ends
wartime cabinet system. The War of Independence begins in
Ireland and Lloyd George calls for volunteers called the 'Black
and Tans' to aid the Royal Irish Constabulary.

1920   He attends San Remo Conference and heads off Churchill's wish for
war with Russia. He attempts to form new centre party by fusing
Coalition Liberals with moderate Conservatives. Parliament
passes the Government of Ireland Act; Southern and Northern
Ireland are to each have their own parliament.

1921   He averts a major strike demanded by Triple Alliance of miners,
dockers and railwaymen. He is dismayed by resignation of
Bonar Law as leader of the Conservative Party. In December he
negotiates the Anglo-Irish Agreement that sets up the Irish Free
State. USA, British Empire, France and Japan sign Washington
Naval Treaty.

History	Culture
Communist Revolt in Berlin.	Bauhaus movement founded by
Paris Peace Conference adopts principle of	Walter Gropius.
founding League of Nations.	Kandinsky, *Dreamy Improvisation.*
Benito Mussolini founds fascist movement	Paul Klee, *Dream Birds.*
in Italy.	Thomas Hardy, *Collected Poems.*
Peace Treaty of Versailles signed.	Herman Hesse, *Demian.*
Britain and France authorise resumption of	George Bernard Shaw, *Heartbreak*
commercial relations with Germany.	*House.*
British-Persian agreement at Tehran to	Eugene D'Albert,
preserve integrity of Persia.	*Revolutionshochzeit.*
US Senate votes against ratification of	Edward Elgar, *Concerto in E Minor*
Versailles Treaty, leaving the USA	*for Cello.*
outside the League of Nations.	Manuel de Falla, *The Three-*
	Cornered Hat.
	Film: *The Cabinet of Dr Caligari.*
League of Nations comes into existence.	F Scott Fitzgerald, *This Side of*
The Hague is selected as seat of	*Paradise.*
International Court of Justice.	Franz Kafka, *The Country Doctor.*
League of Nations headquarters moved to	Katherine Mansfield, *Bliss.*
Geneva.	Rambert School of Ballet formed.
Warren G Harding wins US Presidential	Lyonel Feininger, *Church.*
election.	Juan Gris, *Book and Newspaper.*
Bolsheviks win Russian Civil War.	Vincent D'Indy, *The Legend Of St*
Adolf Hitler announces his 25-point	*Christopher.*
programme in Munich.	Maurice Ravel, *La Valse.*
Paris Conference of wartime allies fixes	Braque, *Still Life with Guitar.*
Germany's reparation payments.	Max Ernst, *The Elephant Celebes.*
Peace treaty signed between Russia and	Aldous Huxley, *Chrome Yellow.*
Germany.	D H Lawrence, *Women in Love.*
State of Emergency proclaimed in	John Dos Passos, *Three Soldiers.*
Germany in the face of economic crisis.	Salzburg Festival established.
	Arthur Honegger, *Le Roi David.*
	Prokofiev, *The Love for Three*
	Oranges.

1922   He receives huge criticism in the press for the Honours scandal and the 'Geddes' axe'. He almost causes war over Chanak in Turkey and Bonar Law writes in *The Times* 'that Britain alone cannot act as 'policeman of the world'. On 19 October the Coalition is voted out by Conservative backbenchers and Lloyd George resigns. 19 October: Lloyd George leaves office, having served five years and 317 days as premier.

History

Britain recognises Kingdom of Egypt under Fuad I.

Gandhi sentenced to six years in prison for civil disobedience.

Election in Irish Free State gives majority to Pro-Treaty candidates. IRA takes large areas under its control.

League of Nations council approves mandates for the former German colonies Togo, the Cameroons and Tanzania, and Palestine.

British mandate proclaimed in Palestine while Arabs declare a day of mourning.

Culture

T S Eliot, *The Waste Land.*

James Joyce, *Ulysses.*

F Scott Fitzgerald, *The Beautiful and Damned.*

Hermann Hesse, *Siddartha.*

Max Beckmann, *Before the Bell.*

Clive Bell, *Since Cezanne.*

Arnold Bax, *Symphony No. 1.*

Irving Berlin, *April Showers.*

British Broadcasting Company (later Corporation) (BBC) founded: first radio broadcasts.

Film: *Dr. Mabuse the Gambler.*

FURTHER READING

A full bibliography of David Lloyd George would make a book of its own and it would be presumptuous of me to attempt anything like one. My most useful service is to direct the reader towards the sources annotated very readably by John Grigg in the first three volumes of his magnificent biography of Lloyd George published between 1973 and 2002. He died just before the publication of the fourth volume so it lacks a sources section. The volumes are: *The Young Lloyd George, The People's Champion 1902–1911, From Peace to War 1912–1916, War Leader 1916–1918*, all republished by Penguin in 2002–3. These, of course, only cover the first 53 years of Lloyd George's long life and for sources on the remainder I recommend Peter Rowland's one-volume biography *David Lloyd George*, published by Macmillan in 1976. Otherwise, I list here the books that I have found most helpful.

'The student of these years can save himself a lot of unnecessary reading if he confines himself to Grigg', wrote the historian Robert Blake. One of the tremendous strengths of this four-volume biography is that it provides a full context to Ll-G's life. Grigg recommended Peter Rowland's *David Lloyd George* as the best one-volume biography, a long read at 900 pages but worth it. Downsizing further, I recommend the 25,000-word biographical essay by Kenneth Morgan in the *Dictionary of National Biography*.

On specialised themes or eras, I found authoritative Kenneth Morgan, *The Age of Lloyd George, The Liberal Party and British Politics, 1890–1929* (George Allen & Unwin, London: 1978); it contains over 100 pages of selected documents. Margaret

MacMillan's *Peacemakers, The Paris Conference of 1919 and Its Attempt to End War* (John Murray, London: 2002) is both comprehensive and entertaining. Incidentally, she completed Grigg's fourth volume of biography that ended otherwise in October 1918. Another thorough and pleasingly opinionated study is John Campbell's *Lloyd George, The Goat in the Wilderness 1922–1931* (Jonathan Cape, London: 1977). Finally, on Lloyd George in the Second World War, I found important, as ever, Paul Addison's *The Road to 1945* (Quartet, London: 1977).

For general background I relied on A J P Taylor's outstanding *English History 1914–1945* (Penguin, London: 1975) and also on his *The First World War* (Penguin, London: 1966). David and Gareth Butler's *Twentieth Century British Political Facts 1900 – 2000* is an indispensable reference (Macmillan, London: 2000).

Primary material: The two main archives for Lloyd George students are the Lloyd George papers, now in the House of Lords Record Office, and the collection of family papers in the National Library of Wales. I found readable but very partial Ll-G's *War Memoirs*, the two volume *popular edition* (Ll-G) published by Odhams, London, in 1938. Also very readable, like most diaries, is Frances Stevenson's *Lloyd George, a Diary,* edited by A J P Taylor and published in 1971. *The Years That Are Past* (Hutchinson, London: 1967), also by Frances Stevenson, is a little thin. *The Diary of Beatrice Webb* Vol 3 (Virago, London: 1984) is a useful corrective as she disliked Ll-G and all that he stood for.

PICTURE SOURCES

INDEX